SKORZENY

By the same author:

Bloody Aachen   Forty-Eight Hours to Hammelburg
Massacre at Malmédy   The Battle of the Ruhr Pocket
Hitler's Werewolves   The Hunt for Martin Bormann
The End of the War   The War in the Shadows
Hunters from the Sky   Operation Stalag
A Bridge at Arnhem   The Battle of Hurtgen Forest
Decision at St Vith   The March on London
The Battle for Twelveland   Operation Northbound
Operation Africa   Bounce the Rhine
The Three-Star Blitz   Siegfried: The Nazis' Last Stand
The Last Assault   Death on a Distant Frontier

SKORZENY

'The Most Dangerous Man in Europe'

by

CHARLES WHITING

Pen & Sword
MILITARY

First published in Great Britain in 1998 by
LEO COOPER
Reprinted in this format in 2010 by
Pen & Sword Military
an imprint of
Pen & Sword Books Ltd
47 Church Street
Barnsley
South Yorkshire   S70 2AS

ISBN 978 1 84884 296 0

The right of Charles Whiting to be identified as
author of this work has been asserted by him in accordance
with the Copyright, Designs and Patents Act 1988

A CIP catalogue record for this book is
available from the British Library

Printed and bound in England
by CPI Antony Rowe, Chippenham, Wiltshire

Pen & Sword Books Ltd incorporates the imprints of
Pen & Sword Aviation, Pen & Sword Maritime, Pen & Sword Military,
Wharncliffe Local History, Pen & Sword Select,
Pen & Sword Military Classics and Leo Cooper,
Remember When, Seaforth Publishing and Frontline Publishing

For a complete list of Pen & Sword titles please contact
PEN & SWORD BOOKS LIMITED
47 Church Street, Barnsley, South Yorkshire, S70 2AS, England
E-mail: enquiries@pen-and-sword.co.uk
Website: www.pen-and-sword.co.uk

Contents

Contents

Author's Note

'There's been a sudden change of plan,' the little doctor with cropped blond hair whispered to me in his Southern German accent. A minute before, he had arrived unexpectedly at the bustling German provincial station, now crowded with early morning commuters, carrying their bulging briefcases, most filled with their 'second breakfast', the eleven o'clock snack that most German office workers eat. The day before he had arranged this journey for me I was to travel alone to the appointed rendezvous with the 'great man', as he called him. Now, surprisingly, he had turned up himself on this cold winter's morning and announced that he was going with me. Was it all part of some real-life cat-and-mouse game. After all the *Herr Doktor*, like others of his kind that I'd met in the Federal Republic, were working on the fringes of legality. Or was it just play-acting on his part? After all, this strange war-in-the-shadows, of which the 'Great Man' was a part, had been going on for well over a quarter of a century now, ever since Germany had lost the war.

As we got into a second class compartment of the express and headed north – 'Might meet somebody in first class that we don't want to see' – the doctor told me that there'd been a change of rendezvous as well. Instead of Hamburg, to which I had thought I was travelling an hour earlier, we were going to Harburg, a small town on the other side of the River Elbe from Hamburg. I understood, didn't I? The man I was anxious to interview was still wanted in the Federal Republic, and had been for a quarter of a century. The German authorities didn't want him in the

I

land of the 'hard D-mark'. After all, he spelled trouble wherever he went. We didn't want any trouble with the *Polizei*, did we? I agreed. Besides, the 'Reds' – the *Herr Doktor* still used words like that – would dearly love to get their hands on him. If they did, they'd probably give him a show trial. I did understand, didn't I? I did.

An hour later we reached Harburg. Outside the rundown station a black BMW was waiting for us, its engine already running. I noted that it didn't have local plates. In addition the driver didn't introduce himself, something unusual in so formal a country as Germany.

But he took off like a bat out of hell and we were driven round and round Harburg. I began to recognize the same places. Obviously the driver was checking to see whether he was being tailed. Finally he was satisfied, dropped us off in a nondescript street and sped away.

The flat – in fact there were two of them, for reasons I could never fathom, for these people obviously didn't live there – was crowded with middle-aged men in shabby suits. Most were obviously foreigners, to judge from their accents, and they looked wary. Although it was only ten o'clock, they were drinking whisky and German *Sekt* (champagne) at an alarming rate. I waited impatiently, feeling decidedly out of place in this crowded room, where no introductions were given or asked for, wondering what would happen next.

Finally, whoever was in charge – I never discovered who he was – decided that everything was safe. 'They' had been thrown off the scent. He made a telephone call and moments later, as if by magic, a small fleet of cars appeared in the street below. We were whisked into them and we were off. Behind us tagged a battered Volkswagen 'Beetle'. This was the 'tail-end Charlie', checking whether we were being followed.

As we crossed the bridge into Hamburg I learned the reason for the Great Man's presence in West Germany. In Madrid, which had been his base since he had fled from an internment camp into exile after the war, his doctors had found a tumour on his spine. It had to be removed immediately, but the Spanish doctors thought it was too tricky an operation for them and told him that the best place to have the tumour removed would be in Germany. Naturally he ran the risk of arrest there, but he was prepared to take the risk. He had been running risks all his life. General Eisenhower, when he was Supreme Allied Commander, had once called him 'public enemy number one' and the 'most dangerous man in Europe'. Now he lay in an upper storey hospital bed in a private room well away from the rest of the '*Klinik*', guarded by his ex-commandos who had come from all over Western Europe to guard their old C.O. He was obviously a very sick man. He had lost a great deal of weight and had now turned a strange unhealthy light yellow colour. But his broad face, criss-crossed with the sabre scars of his Viennese youth, still had that challenging look that I remembered from the wartime photos taken at the time when his exploits had made him world-famous – some would say infamous.

'Skorzeny,' he said, with a soft Viennese lilt in his voice. He offered me a weak hand and even attempted the traditional Austrian bow from the shoulders. He was obviously not surprised by my visit.

Suddenly I remembered that freezing December day in 1944 when I, with a bunch of other boys in uniform, had been rushed to guard a crossroads in the frozen Belgian countryside. Behind us we had left panic. The Sergeant-Major had 'gone on the trot' – deserted; officers were burning secret documents in the courtyard; NCOs were busy breaking bottles of beer and whisky – 'We don't want the troops to start looting and drinking *now*' – against the walls; drafts were being assembled everywhere for dispatch to the front. The great flap started.

And it had been all due to this man in the hospital bed. Then, according to the wild rumours circulating right up to Supreme Headquarters back in Versailles, the men of Skorzeny's secret *Jagdkommando* (Hunting Commando) were everywhere, dressed in American uniforms and driving captured jeeps. Everyone was suspect. At the roadblocks the defenders were ordered to shoot

3

first and ask questions later, something which happened all too frequently that December. Now, here in front of me on the white cot, weak and ill, was the man who had masterminded that operation – one of the greatest psychological victories on any side in the whole of the Second World War.

Now he faced his last battle. The German doctors had just discovered that he had two tumours on his spine, one above the other. He was paralyzed from the waist down. 'I thought he would be so discouraged that he'd just give up', recalled Heinz Wirmer, one of his former SS commandos who had accompanied him from Madrid. But that wasn't to be. 'He certainly surprised me,' Wirmer said later. 'Within hours of regaining consciousness, he was hollering for a therapist and vowing that he would talk again.' Which indeed he did and continued to do so for another five years until his death in 1975.

Skorzeny's determination was typical. For most of the war, after he had been invalided out of the SS Division 'Adolf Hitler Bodyguard' as unfit for further active service in 1941 – how ironic that appeared in retrospect – Skorzeny had fought a bitter war in the shadows. He and his men had battled in a dozen different countries in three continents. They had attempted to kill the Yugoslav partisan leader, Tito; they had successfully rescued the Fascist dictator Mussolini from his mountain prison; Hungary had been kept in the war as Germany's reluctant ally by their kidnapping of the Hungarian dictator Admiral Horthy's son.

Spectacular new secret weapons had been employed for the first time in warfare. It had been planned that forerunners of the Anglo-American Polaris submarines – U-boats armed with V-2 rockets – would attack New York. In December, 1944, Skorzeny's efforts had made possible the first 'cruise missile' raid – Heinkel bombers carrying V-1 'doodlebugs' to be launched from the North Sea at targets on Britain's west coast. There had been silenced sub-machine guns, rifles that fired round corners, battle mines launched by frogmen against Allied-built combat bridges across the Rhine, including the most famous of them all, the one at Remagen.

Once Skorzeny and his paras of the *Jagdkommando* had attempted to bring the war to an end by the assassination of the three great Allied leaders, Churchill, Roosevelt and Stalin, in Persia in 1943. Even when it was clear that the '1,000 Year Reich' was almost defeated, Skorzeny's spies, saboteurs and assassins made a determined attempt on the life of the Supreme Commander himself, so that a hard-pressed Eisenhower was confined to his HQ under heavy guard for days on end. Otto Skorzeny apparently never gave up, even when he was facing almost certain death as he was in Hamburg-Boberg that month.

Naturally the men of the *Jagdkommando* often paid the ultimate price for their daring, though the middle-aged former commandos assembled at the hospital, risking financial loss and perhaps even their freedom for having done so, did not seem to hold it against their former commander. In a way they were heroes – Churchill even praised Skorzeny's daring rescue of Mussolini in 1943 in the House of Commons. But they were also victims. Young men, dropped by parachute miles behind the enemy lines, to die alone and abandoned in the snow-bound Russian wilderness. In one case, a Russian-speaking *Jagdkommando* took four months to cover 200 miles of Russian-held territory to return successfully to base. Others were hunted like wild animals through the Rumanian mountains and clubbed to death when caught. Just like the modern British SAS troopers, they were young men who knew how to live off the land, think for themselves and never be daunted by the disastrous mess they often found themselves in.

Sometimes one would have wished these bold young men a better fate. Take the case of those three Skorzeny saboteurs, dressed as pseudo-Americans and captured behind US lines in the Ardennes in the third week of December, 1944. Sentenced to death by their American captors, they pleaded for mercy. 'We have been captured by the Americans,' they wrote in their appeal for clemency, 'without having fired a single shot, because we did not wish to become murderers. We were sentenced to death and we are now dying for criminals who have not only us but also – and what is worse – our families on their conscience.'

Their plea didn't help. On the morning of 23 December, 1944, they were placed against a wall in Belgium (one can still see the bullet marks made by the firing squad to this day) and shot. After all spying and sabotage are dangerous games.

These unfortunates remain a minor footnote in the history of the Second World War, unlike their commander, Otto Skorzeny, who evolved a technique of clandestine warfare which has still not yet been equalled by any other secret service in the world (with, perhaps, the exception of the KGB and the Israeli *Mossad*, though details of their operations are hard to pin down). Instead of the kind of operations carried out by, say, the world-famous British SAS, which deals with strictly military targets, Skorzeny aimed higher.

His theory was 'Go for the head not for the guts'. In other words, take out the brain and the body politic will collapse of its own accord. He operated at the highest level. Take, for instance, the operations he carried out in relation to Mussolini, Tito and Horthy and the ones he planned against Stalin, Churchill, Roosevelt* and Eisenhower. In the first three instances, the success of his efforts resulted in the continuation of the war between Hungary and Russia in the East and the formation of a new Fascist republic in Italy in the West under Mussolini, again leading to the continuation of the war in that unfortunate country for two years after Italy had surrendered to the Allies. Unlike David Stirling, the founder of the SAS, Skorzeny wanted to achieve not just limited military results but vitally important political ones as well.

Skorzeny's brief wartime career in overt operations, just two and a half years in all, marked a milestone in the war in the

* Hitler was strictly opposed to attempts being made on the lives of enemy leaders. In 1943 he lifted that restriction and in that year a plane supposedly carrying Churchill from North Africa to the UK was shot down. It was the wrong plane but the hand of Skorzeny was clearly visible behind that operation. The principal victim then was the movie star Leslie Howard.

shadows. His major political successes put him in a class of his own. But these major coups bore with them the seeds of his own personal defeats. Thereafter he could never settle down to the life of an ordinary engineer for which he had been trained. Covert ops, if possible at the highest level, would henceforth dominate his life, even when he was old and sick. After 1945 when everyone else wanted to forget the Second World War, Skorzeny would always be on the run, not only for what he had done during the war but also for his undercover activities thereafter. He would have to keep on running almost to the day he died. But never again would there be anyone else like this scarfaced Austrian giant. For he did what was given to only a few men. *He helped to change the course of the Second World War.*

I

The Man

The situation at the little Belgian town of Dinant, poised on the clifflike bank of the River Meuse, was tense on the evening of 23 December, 1944. On that chill day, the shortest day of the year, a scratch force of British armoured troops from the 29th Armoured Brigade, negro GIs from the US Service Corps and a mixed group of engineers, US MPs and untrained Army Air Corps men was prepared to meet the thrust of the German XLVII Panzer Korps presently driving through the Ardennes for the vital bridges across the Meuse. The Battle of the Bulge was exactly seven days old and everywhere the Germans seemed to be victorious, sweeping all opposition in front of them in their vigorous attack to the last great water barrier before the vital Allied supply port of Antwerp, their target. Once they had captured the bridges across the River Meuse at Huy and Dinant, there seemed little likelihood that the depleted Allied Armies could stop them in their drive across the flat Belgian plain. It would be 1940 all over again.

Now, in Dinant, squeezed in along the strip of flat land on the eastern bank of the river, the scratch Anglo-American force under Colonel A. W. Brown DSO nervously awaited the arrival of the Germans. Colonel Brown knew that his men would be hardly a match for the elite German troops. His British armour was antiquated and badly worn out from six months of campaigning. In fact, the 29th Armoured Brigade had been rushed to the front from the supply depot where they had been in the midst of exchanging the beat-up Shermans they had driven through

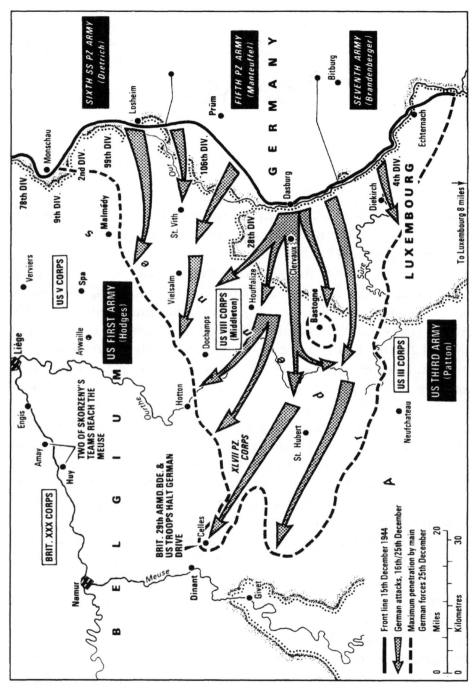

The Battle of the Bulge

France for the heavier-gunned, faster Firefly. As for his 'infantry', most of the Americans had received six weeks' basic infantry training in the States a year or so before and then gone straight into technical trades, forgetting all about tactics and infantry skills. Besides, apart from a few Bazookas and machine guns, they had no heavy weapons whatsoever.

Looking at his situation on that day, Brown concluded that his real defence rested in the bridge which spanned the river. He issued the order that it was to be blown as soon as the enemy appeared, but only on a specific order from him personally. Meanwhile he reasoned that the German armour would probably approach the town from the south, entering it by the road. Fortunately, at one spot this road was ideally suited for defence, even by relatively unskilled troops, as it passed through an opening cut through solid rock. He ordered his engineers to string a necklace of Hawkins mines across the road which would stop most vehicles, even armoured ones. Before this barrier, he set up an infantry-armoured checkpoint. If any vehicle refused to stop at the checkpoint, the Hawkins mines would ensure that it came to a halt shortly afterwards.

Thus the little garrison waited tensely for the coming assault. But as the hours passed no German armour made its appearance. The night was silent save for the ever-present noise of war in the background – the rumble of the heavy guns somewhere up at the front. Soon it would be midnight, and the start of Christmas Eve.

Then there was the sound of a motor. At their checkpoint the waiting infantry gripped their weapons. Was this the German attack?

Suddenly, before they could stop it, a US jeep containing four men came barrelling up to the checkpoint. In an instant it had crashed through and was roaring on down the road towards Dinant. But not for long. One minute later it had driven over the chain of Hawkins grenades. In a thick crump of heavy explosive and a sheet of violent flame, the jeep came to an abrupt halt. Swiftly the alarmed Anglo-American troops rushed to the spot. Among the smoking wreckage of the little Allied vehicle, four men lay sprawled out. They were dressed in American uniforms.

For one horrified moment the soldiers stopped in their tracks. Had they inadvertently killed four of their own men? Someone bent down to examine the bodies more carefully. With the aid of a dimmed flashlight, he opened the olive-drab coat of the first man, buttoned up tightly to the neck. On the dead man's collars gleamed the silver runes of the German SS. The dead men were German.

The surprise experienced by that little group of shocked soldiers at midnight on 23 December, 1944, was one shared by similar groups everywhere along the eighty-mile Ardennes front during those first days of the Battle of the Bulge. From all sides the alarming reports started to flood into regimental and divisional headquarters. Disguised German soldiers were reported at Huy (also situated near a vital Meuse bridge); 'American' Shermans manned by 'American' GIs up at the point of SS *Obersturmbannführer* Peiper's Battle Group of the 1st SS Panzer Division; 'American' Signal Corps men discovered trying to cut the main line between First Army and 12th Army Group. And the reports were not just confined to the front. In Paris it was reported that some three hundred German paratroopers disguised in American uniform were rallying on the Café de la Paix from where they would attack the headquarters of the Supreme Commander General Eisenhower himself. In far off Brittany peasants confidently reported large scale paradrops of German troops in Anglo-American uniforms and even in London a rumour went the rounds that disguised Germans had penetrated the numerous German POW camps in the country and were preparing a large-scale uprising which would disrupt the whole Allied rear echelon.

As the first week of the German surprise offensive began to draw to its close it was clear that the Allied rear areas were in the grip of one of the greatest spy and saboteur scares in the whole history of war. Operation *Greif*, planned so hurriedly in

Berlin two months earlier that it had seemed doomed to failure from the start, was an outstanding success, perhaps the only real German success of the gigantic land battle waged in the snowy forests of the Ardennes. *Obersturmbannführer* Otto Skorzeny had pulled off yet another of his amazing coups. The man whom the frustrated Americans were soon to call 'the most dangerous man in Europe' had done it again.

There was little in Otto Skorzeny's early life to give a clue as to why he should become the 'most dangerous man in Europe'. He was born on 12 June, 1908, into a typical middle-class Viennese family, his name pointing to the fact that his forefathers had Slavic origins.

Naturally this well-to-do Austrian family, like most of their compatriots, suffered in the 'bad years' after the First World War when the Austrian currency was worth hardly the paper it was printed on, and the Skorzeny children survived only because of the efforts of the International Red Cross. Otto's boyhood ran through the worst years of the Depression and he remembers his father, whose practice as an engineer had suffered through lack of capital and the lack of value of the Austrian Schilling, impressing upon him the need for self-discipline. Tasting butter for the first time when he was fifteen, his father told him that there was 'no harm in doing without things; it might even be a good thing not to get used to a soft life'. It was advice and training that were to come in useful to the teenager who was beginning to grow into a giant. (In later life he was six foot four and broadly built.)

But perhaps it was his first encounter with the traditional student duelling societies of the University of Vienna, at which he enrolled to study engineering at the age of eighteen, which marked the first decisive influence on his life. For over a century and a half German-speaking universities had cultivated the art of duelling with the sabre. The University of Vienna was no exception. *Schlagende Verbindungen*, or duelling societies, flourished and young Otto Skorzeny was soon an enthusiastic member of one such society which met in the outlying cafés of surburban Vienna, complete with ritualistic duelling and gigantic drinking bouts.

Otto Skorzeny fought his first duel in the year he entered the university. It was a nerve-wracking business and as he confessed years later in his memoirs: 'I could feel my heart beating rapidly. I could only see the face of my opponent very vaguely through the steel grill of my mask. Blade against blade! . . . With only the occasional pause while the blade of my sabre was disinfected . . . Then suddenly after the seventh round I felt a short, sharp blow on my head. Surprisingly enough it didn't hurt too much. My only fear was that I had flinched.' He had not.

Thereafter the young student fought thirteen more duels which resulted in his achieving the *Schmisse*, the scars, which were to decorate his cheek for the rest of his life and gain him the title of 'Scarface' in American quarters during the Second World War. But for Otto Skorzeny duelling was more than just obtaining the much sought after *Schmisse*. As he was to comment later: 'I was often grateful later for the self-discipline we learned in our student club. I never felt so bad under fire as I did at eighteen when I had to fight my first duel under the sharp eyes of my fellow students. My knowledge of pain, learned with the sabre, taught me not to be afraid of fear. And just as in duelling you must fix your mind on striking at the enemy's head, so, too, in war. You cannot waste time on feinting and sidestepping. You must decide on your target and go in.'

When the war came, Austria, part of the Third Reich since the time of the *Anschluss*, was also forced to supply its contribution of men to the German war machine. Not that Skorzeny waited to be conscripted. The successful thirty-one-year-old engineer, who had already built up his own business in Vienna, volunteered immediately for the Luftwaffe, hoping to be commissioned as a pilot – because he had already done much civil flying in single-engined machines.

But he was to be disappointed. He was told after five months' training that he was 'too old'. It appeared that he was fit only for routine ground crew duties. That was too much for him.

Immediately he volunteered for the elite German *Leibstandarte* of the SS, the premier SS division, usually known as 'Hitler's Bodyguard'.

Only twelve of the many who had volunteered were passed and Skorzeny was one of them. Thereafter he was posted to the division's 'moonlight company' named after its CO's unpleasant habit of carrying out most of his training at night. But in spite of being the oldest – of the twelve accepted into the division, Skorzeny made out, with his naturally robust physique, hardened by the years of duelling and sport in the prewar period. Soon he was promoted to the rank of NCO and thereafter to that of *Fähnrich*, a kind of officer-cadet who had to prove himself among the ranks before he became an officer. He was then transferred to the *Waffen* SS division *Das Reich*.

But as his career was to prove, Skorzeny was not meant for routine military duties, even with such an elite formation as the *Das Reich*. In Holland in 1940, just before his promotion to second-lieutenant, he was in a café drinking schnapps with several companions from the division when he took objection to a portrait of Prince Bernhard of the Netherlands hanging on the wall. As a young man, the German-born prince had served in the SS himself, and Skorzeny now regarded him as a traitor because he had fled to London with the exiled Dutch government. 'Take that picture, down', he ordered the Dutch café owner.

The stubborn and patriotic Dutchman refused.

'If you don't take it down soon,' Skorzeny threatened, 'I'll shoot it down.'

Still the Dutchman would not do as he was commanded.

Skorzeny did not hesitate. Drawing his pistol, he took aim and fired at the cord holding up the portrait. His first shot was sufficient. The picture fell to the floor, the glass shattered, and the drunken party went on.

The incident had its consequences. The Dutchman reported what had happened to Skorzeny's commander and the marksman found himself on the carpet before an angry CO anxious to ensure good relations with the newly conquered Dutch. His promotion was stopped and he found himself confined to barracks for six weeks.

The incident confirmed Skorzeny, as did many other such (for him) bureaucratic incidents, in his belief that he did not like ordinary routine military units. But in the years 1940–41 he did not have too much time to reflect upon his dislike of 'channels' and 'barrack-room bull'. Events were moving too quickly. In rapid succession he took part in the Balkan campaign, the march into Rumania and Hungary, and then in that fateful summer of 1941 the invasion of Russia.

Now he was to have his first real taste of that hard battle which was to form the major component of his daily life for the next four years. The *Das Reich*, as the second SS division, was in the forefront of the battle everywhere; and although Skorzeny was an engineer officer whose main task was to keep the division's tanks and tracked vehicles moving, he saw his share of action. Soon he had won his first award for bravery, one of the many which were to make him one of the most decorated soldiers in Hitler's Germany.

Then, in the last major German offensive of the winter of 1941, Skorzeny was chatting with two fellow officers in the shelter of a Russian peasant house some two hundred yards from the front line when they heard the sound of one of the feared Russian *Stalinorgel* – 'Stalin's organs' – a noise like canvas being ripped. One, two, three . . . the shells hurtled down all about the cowering SS officers. Suddenly Skorzeny felt a great blow on the back of his head and blacked out.

When he came to, a soldier handed him a cigarette and started to brush the earth from him. Skorzeny, his head ringing, puffed gratefully at the cigarette, not realizing that his wound was going to plague him for many years to come. Refusing any real attention save a glass of schnapps and a few aspirins, he went on with his duties and continued to do so until December of that year, when the continual headaches and a bad case of stomach colic made it clear that he would have to be evacuated to Germany for specialized treatment. Skorzeny did not know, as he said goodbye to his comrades and promised he would soon be back among them, that his days with a regular military formation were over. As the hospital train carried him and the other survivors of the unsuccessful winter offensive through the wastes of Russia, into Poland and home to Germany, Skorzeny was heading for a spectacularly unorthodox military career which even in his wildest dreams he could never have believed would be his.

In December, 1941, when he was transferred to Vienna in a weak state of health, he returned with the Iron Cross and an illness which was to pursue him for years to come, even into the Allied POW camps. Behind him (as Charles Foley, one of his biographers has written), 'he had left his copy of the *Seven Pillars* [surely a hint of what was soon to come] and the last of his illusions; the fires of the Eastern front which steeled his character also magnetized it against shams.'

In the early weeks of 1942 Skorzeny returned to Berlin to serve in the depot of the *Leibstandarte*, being in charge of the technical services there. But the depot was an anticlimax after the action and the camaraderie of the front. For six months he stuck it out, keeping busy enough with the job of helping to transfer the lst SS from an infantry or semi-motorized division to a complete, fully armoured division. Then one day he was asked to report to the HQ of the *Waffen* SS.

A little puzzled by the summons, Skorzeny dutifully reported and listened attentively as the high-ranking officer behind the desk told him that the SS needed 'a technically trained officer' who would be prepared to 'carry out special duties'. He pricked up his ears. Was this a chance of getting out of his routine duties at the depot?

The officer explained that the time had come for Germany to set up commando troops on the same lines as the British who had successfully initiated this type of irregular warfare when she had been unable to attack the enemy with large-scale formations. Now, in the middle years of the war, Germany was finally also beginning to feel the pinch. With most of her regular formations bottled up in Russia there was scope for highly skilled small groups of brave men who could carry the war to the enemy in unexpected areas. This would not only shake the enemy from his growing sense of superiority but would also spread fear and alarm altogether out of proportion to the effort expended.

Skorzeny did not take long to make up his mind, although he reasoned that he had been offered the job because no career officer in the regular Wehrmacht would touch it or because the High Command would not allow career officers to apply for it in case they became puffed up with their own importance at the grandiose prospects offered by this post and the 'carte blanche' that went with it. And there was nothing subtle in his reasons for accepting: 'For anyone with blood in his veins,' he explained later, 'there is, at certain turning points, only one way to go. A man who can still see the choice of two roads then may be a clever fellow – I could not say much more for him.'

Thus it was that, on 18 April, 1943, Otto Skorzeny, newly promoted to the rank of *Hauptsturmführer der Reserve*, became head of Germany's first special troops, the *Friedenthaler Jadgverbande* (Friedenthal Hunting Groups) named after their place of training, Friedenthal, near Berlin. The momentous career of Germany's 'Commando Extraordinary' had begun.

2

Early days

When Otto Skorzeny got down to looking at the men and equipment available to him that spring, he soon realized that the future of Germany's first commando troops was none too bright.

At first he had at his disposal only about a company of soldiers, albeit all front-experienced, under the command of a Dutch captain who had gone over to the Waffen SS. His special equipment was virtually nil, save for a few captured enemy weapons and bits and pieces of other equipment and clothing. Such standard British commando tools as machine pistols fitted with silencers, plastic explosive, cliff-scaling rocket apparatus etc simply did not exist, and from all reports, Skorzeny did not believe that Adolf Hitler would tolerate the hard-pressed German war industry 'wasting' its time on such 'fancy gadgets'.

But Skorzeny was not easily put off. In fact, it was one of his outstanding characteristics that he did not believe in defeat or fear, following that Nietzsche quotation which became his motto for the next few years: 'live dangerously'.

Already Schellenberg, the smart young SS general and secret serviceman who was his nominal chief, was pressing him to embark on the first commando raid and impress Hitler with the future of this new organization. Quickly he started to assemble the men he needed for his special operations. Firstly he recruited an old friend from his Viennese student days, Karl Radl, now an army captain, who would remain with him for the rest of the war as a highly capable adjutant.

To support Radl he enlisted the services of two other young

men who had just graduated and were preparing to enter the secret service. They were happy to join him, excited at the prospects offered to the unconventional commando troops. Then he looked around for the rank and file. He acquired them from various sources: many from the SS Parachute Battalion; others from the secret special service Brandenburg Infantry Battalion, which supplied highly skilled parachutists who were also mostly linguists; and a few volunteers from the ranks of the normal *Waffen* SS. In the end Skorzeny had the equivalent of two battalions of highly trained, enthusiastic young men, convinced one hundred per cent of the Nazi cause and recruited from a half dozen different European countries so that all the major European languages from Russian to English were represented in the ranks. An ideal outfit for the task ahead.

But Skorzeny was not satisfied. He did not feel his men were up to the high standard set by the British commandos. Above all he needed the latter's special equipment. For two weeks he immersed himself in captured commando and resistance documents, going through them with the aid of a dictionary (at that time he remembered little of his school English, though one day he would re-learn the language fluently), giving himself a crash course in the British methods. Then he went to Holland where the German counter-Intelligence agents had penetrated the Dutch Resistance either by 'bending' double-agents or by liberally spending German gold.

By this time he knew from his study of the captured British documents that Allied planes crossed over to Holland nightly bringing special supplies to the Dutch Underground. Swiftly he set to work to ensure that the British would also supply his own form of resistance – the Friedenthal (it means 'valley of peace') Commando. Using the Dutch double agents in German pay he rapidly accumulated special British equipment which he would use later in his own commando missions. Highly delighted and amused by the whole scheme of deception, he waited up night after night for the British planes to come droning in with a fresh supply of plastic explosives, Hawkins mines, Stens, radio sets and machine pistols armed with silencers. With one such weapon, a silenced Sten, he shot a duck on a lake in front of a group of astonished Wehrmacht officers who did not believe such a thing was possible. Predictably Hitler prohibited the mass production of the British weapon. Nothing, in the Führer's opinion, was better than German weapons; hence no silenced Stens were made in Germany.

Meanwhile his unit was developing at the hunting lodge at Friedenthal, his headquarters, set in a vast park amid several acres of remote woodlands. A barracks, more correctly a series of wooden huts, had begun to go up, and volunteers were pouring in, including more and more parachutists–linguists from the *Brandenburg* who were dissatisfied with the use of their specialist formation as a normal infantry outfit.

Moreover Schellenberg was again pressing that the commandos should move. Quickly Skorzeny planned an operation to cut off the Allied supply route to a hard-pressed Russia through Persia. Already a German officer had been smuggled into the country and had made contact with the mountain tribes who would be only too glad to wage a guerrilla war against the Anglo-American supply columns if the Germans would give them gifts of the much coveted silver- and gold-adorned rifles and swords.

Radl was dispatched to Berlin to do the rounds of the capital's antique shops, ransacking them of their ancient fowling pieces and inlaid muskets, but hardly had he returned to Friedenthal when the project was cancelled because the German High Command refused to loan Skorzeny a long-distance transport plane to parachute them to the tribes.

But Skorzeny and Radl had little time to think of the wasted effort. Hardly had the latter returned to Friedenthal when Skorzeny was informed by Schellenberg, acting on Himmler's orders, that the chief of the SS wanted a raid launched on the town of Magnitogorsk, some thousand miles away in the Russian Urals. Apparently the vital Soviet war industry was out of range of German bombers except for the four-engined Kondor, and Himmler had hit on the idea of using the new Skorzeny Commando unit to put the important blast furnaces at Magnitogorsk out of action. Skorzeny set to work immediately on this new project which bore the cover name 'Operation Ulm', but he soon found that, in spite of the many reconnaissance photos supplied by the Luftwaffe long-range reconnaissance units, German Intelligence knew virtually nothing about Magnitogorsk, or indeed about the whole Ural industrial complex. Sadly he told Radl that he did not think Operation Ulm possible and that he would have to report his findings to Himmler. The mission was impossible.

Radl objected. He told Skorzeny that nothing was to be gained by annoying the 'most powerful man in Europe'; the commando might have need of SS Führer Heinrich Himmler in the months to come. Schellenberg objected too. The smooth cynical SS man told Skorzeny: 'The more absurd the idea put to you by a really important person, the more rapturously you should welcome it. Showy preparation should be started forthwith; assurances must be incessantly given that plans are advancing apace. Then gradually, drop by drop, the notion that certain outside factors may defer the glorious consummation may be allowed to seep through, until the author of the project finds himself wondering at his own earlier enthusiasm and begins discreetly to shelve the whole thing, if he has not forgotten all about it already.'

Thus the months began to tick by with many starts and no ends. Slowly Skorzeny started to understand the role he and his men were going to play in the rest of the war. His brief when he had taken over in April had been to 'undertake military commando missions and acts of sabotage with the aid of agents'. He naturally inclined towards the 'commando missions' because he was first and foremost a soldier. In addition, the situation of Germany at that time did not encourage the use of agents for 'acts of sabotage'.

As he wrote himself after the war: 'The whole of Europe was occupied by us. Where should we find Americans or Englishmen who were prepared to act as agents for us in their countries? If money were the only attraction one could not expect too much from them.'

In the end Skorzeny concluded that he would concentrate forthwith on strictly military actions, using German soldiers with 'their devotion to duty' aided perhaps by one or two members of the local population.

He would be able to test that conclusion in practice much sooner than he realized.

On 25 July, 1943, Skorzeny was taking his ease, chatting with an old Viennese friend in the Berlin Hotel Eden with his usual glass of cognac in front of him. He was in civilian clothes, relaxed and mentally far away from the war. He knew, however, that he would soon have to report by telephone to Friedenthal HQ. Excusing himself, he rose reluctantly and strolled through the lounge to the nearest telephone kiosk.

His secretary was almost on the verge of panic when he finally contacted her. For two hours the whole base had been searching for him. When he queried why, she yelled: 'Chief, they want you at the Leader's headquarters! A plane is waiting to take off with you at 1700 hours from Tempelhof!'

Skorzeny understood the panic in his secretary's voice. No one had ever been summoned from his unit to the Führer's HQ before. The balloon must really be up!

Quickly he ordered her to tell Radl to come to Berlin. 'Tell Radl to go into my room and pack my uniform and toilet gear. Don't let him forget anything. But haven't you any indication what this is all about?'

'No,' his secretary replied, 'we don't know a thing here.'

His mind racing with a thousand possibilities, Skorzeny hurried to the Berlin city airport. Radl was already there when he arrived, but all he could tell his chief was that there had been some kind of change of government in Italy. Together they strode across to the waiting plane. Once inside, after saying goodbye to Radl, Skorzeny changed into his uniform and settled into the nearest seat (he had the whole VIP plane to himself).

Helping himself to a cognac from the built-in rack of drinks, he strapped himself in and waited for take-off.

Skorzeny had never before been to Hitler's HQ in the East, the 'Wolf's Lair'. He expected the HQ to be a rough-and-ready series of trenches and underground bunkers. It turned out to be a small village of camouflaged huts and bunkers set in the middle of a forest and guarded by a battalion of SS infantry and several score of anti-aircraft guns.

But he had no time to view his new surroundings. He was ushered immediately into an anteroom by one of Hitler's immaculate SS aides. Swiftly the room began to fill up with officers, all senior to him, who had been summoned from all over Europe for some highly important, hush-hush conference.

In the end six of them were ushered into Hitler's room, a simply furnished place, its sole decoration consisting of maps and a sand-table. A moment later Hitler himself entered. The group sprang to attention and were introduced by one of the adjutants.

Then Hitler stepped back a pace and stared along the row of men, still standing rigidly to attention. Suddenly he asked: 'Which of you know Italy?'

Skorzeny, the most junior, was the only one to reply: 'I have travelled through Italy twice, as far as Naples, on my motorcycle.'

Hitler nodded. 'What do you think of the Italians?' he asked the group.

Their answers came hesitantly. 'Axis partners . . . Members of the Anti-Comintern Pact . . . Ally.' When it came to Skorzeny's turn, he snapped: 'I am an Austrian, my Leader.'

He felt the statement should suffice. Hitler, as a fellow Austrian, must realize what he felt about a nation which, in his opinion, had stolen one of the most beautiful parts of Old Austria, the South Tyrol.

Hitler looked at the big Viennese for a long time. Then apparently he made up his mind. 'The other gentlemen can go. I want to speak to you, however, *Hauptsturmführer* Skorzeny.'

1. 'He volunteered for the Elite German Liebstandarte of the SS...
   usually known as Hitler's bodyguard' (p.15). Skorzeny is on the
   extreme left.

2. 'Skorzeny had never before been to Hitler's HQ in the East, the
   "Wolf's Lair"' (p.24). Hitler is seen here with Himmler (second
   from left), Raeder (right) and others.

3. 'Quickly he changed into paratroop tropical uniform' (p.26).

4. Happier days! The caption on this pre-war photograph reads "Adolf Hitler – Benito Mussolini. The guarantee of European peace".

5. The Hotel Campo Imperatore in the Apennines, where Mussolini was held prisoner (see p.32).

6. 'Mussolini, dressed in an overlarge black coat and a broad-brimmed hat...' (p.41).

7. 'All that was left was Captain Gerlach's "Storch" spotter plane' (p.40).

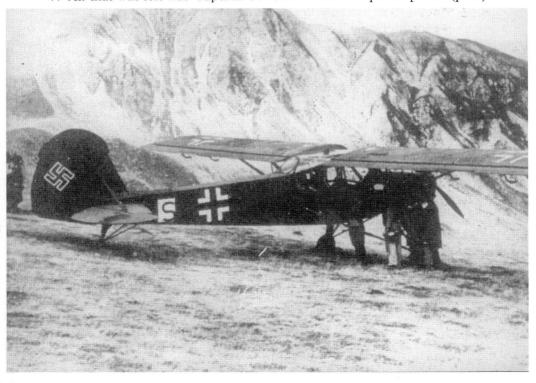

8. 'Today you have carried out a mission which will go down in history, You have given me back my old friend Mussolini' (p.43).

9. 'All were agreed that the ageing Admiral Horthy was very much under the influence of his younger son Miki, the enfant terrible of the family' (p.47).

10. 'We are going to dash across France through the American Army and capture Eisenhower's Headquarters' (p.60). Eisenhower seen here with General Troy Middleton.

11. 'The word went out to look for "the most dangerous man in Europe"' (p.69).

12. 'After two years in a prisoner-of-war camp Skorzeny was brought to trial in Dachau' (p.99).

13. The successful engineering consultant.

14. Evita Peron.
    Skorzeny thought
    that after being in
    prison for several
    months he was the
    ideal man to soften
    her up (see p.110).
    (Corbis-Bettmann).

15. 'General Reinhard
    Gehlen… liked to
    live in the shadows
    and was rarely
    photographed'
    (p.113).

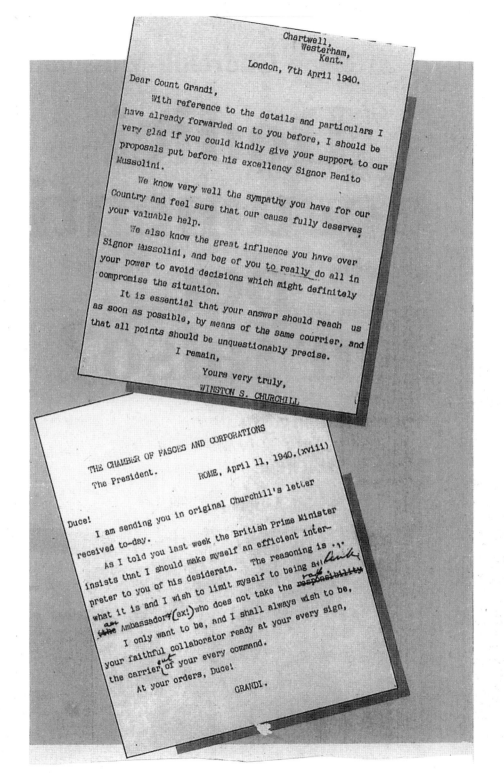

Chartwell,
Westerham,
Kent.
London, 7th April 1940.

Dear Count Grandi,

With reference to the details and particulars I have already forwarded on to you before, I should be very glad if you could kindly give your support to our proposals put before his excellency Signor Benito Mussolini.

We know very well the sympathy you have for our Country and feel sure that our cause fully deserves your valuable help.

We also know the great influence you have over Signor Mussolini, and beg of you to really do all in your power to avoid decisions which might definitely compromise the situation.

It is essential that your answer should reach us as soon as possible, by means of the same courrier, and that all points should be unquestionably precise.

I remain,

Yours very truly,
WINSTON S. CHURCHILL

THE CHAMBER OF FASCES AND CORPORATIONS

The President.   ROME, April 11, 1940.(xviii)

Duce!

I am sending you in original Churchill's letter received to-day.

As I told you last week the British Prime Minister insists that I should make myself an efficient interpreter to you of his desiderata. The reasoning is what it is and I wish to limit myself to being an Ambassador (ex!) who does not take the responsibility.

I only want to be, and I shall always wish to be, your faithful collaborator ready at your every sign, the carrier of your every command.

At your orders, Duce!

GRANDI.

16 & 17. (Over) The 'Churchill Letters' (see pp.134-137).

Rome, the 16th April 1940

Your Excellency,

Count Dino Grandi has informed me about Your intentions of wishing to have, if the worse come to the worst, a friendly Country sitting at the Peace Conference Table, who could safeguard those particular interests of Yours, already mentioned by You.

Will, Your Excellency, nevertheless kindly let me have a detailed memorandum to be submitted before His Majesty the King, in order to obtain His high consent on the matters, as I can already state at this moment that His Majesty's consent and advice will be in the affirmative, because We are rather bothered with Germany, who is insisting to secure a pledge from Us to keep the Three Party Pact alive, which we have wanted before.

Believe me,   MUSSOLINI

His Excellence WINSTON S. CHURCHILL,
London.

Chartwell,
Westerham,
Kent.

London, the 22nd April 1940.

Excellency Benito Mussolini,

I received Your letter 16th inst. and I am very glad to be able to finally know your intentions concerning my Country. On my part I can state after a meeting of the Supreme   and Ministry Government Council that we came to the decision of getting Your support as a Friendly Nation, at the Scheme of Pact hereby Joigned terms.   Your Excellency has given to me to understand that an understanding between Italy and Great Britain should be possible; these are the basis which we propose and which we consider more suitable to the present mutual political conditions. We await an official confirmation for the execution of the Pact, and I wish to remain

Your Obedient Servant,
WINSTON S. CHURCHILL.

While the others filed out, Skorzeny told himself that at least Hitler could pronounce his name correctly, which the others present could not. He felt a little flattered.

When they were alone. Hitler got down to business at once. 'I have a very important commission for you. Mussolini, my friend and our loyal comrade in arms, was betrayed yesterday by his king and arrested by his own countrymen.'

Hitler was referring to the secret surrender negotiations carried out by the Badoglio faction in Italy which had resulted in the Italians starting to surrender to the Allies now ready to land in Italy. One aspect of these negotiations had been the decision of the new 'Badoglio Government' to imprison the Italian Duce who had been head of the Italian state since 1922.

'I cannot and will not leave Italy's greatest son in the lurch,' Hitler continued. 'To me the Duce is the incarnation of the ancient grandeur of Rome. Italy under the new government will desert us. I will keep faith with my old ally and dear friend; he must be rescued promptly or he will be handed over to the Allies.'

Hitler paused and allowed the words to sink in, staring at Skorzeny intently the whole time.

Then he resumed the conversation: 'I herewith order you to carry out the task, which is vital for the war. You must do everything in your power to carry it out. And if you do, then you will be successful.

'Now the main points. You must keep the mission secret. Only five other people apart from yourself must know of it. You will return to the Luftwaffe for the operation. I've already informed General Student [head of the German paratroops who came under the command of the air force]. Discuss the matter with him. He'll give you the details. It's up to you to find out where the Duce is . . . And once again, absolute secrecy . . . I hope to hear from you soon and would like to wish you all the best.'

With that Hitler dismissed him and Skorzeny left the room.

But hardly had he emerged when a Luftwaffe officer snapped 'General Student would like to see you now.'

The Mussolini Rescue Operation was under way.

3

Where is Mussolini?

Rome was peaceful enough when Skorzeny flew in the next day, but unbearably hot. Quickly he changed into paratroop tropical uniform and set about planning the Mussolini rescue operation, aided by Radl who flew to Rome a few days later, together with about sixty selected officers and soldiers from Friedenthal and ten special officers trained in Intelligence services.

Problem number one was, of course, where were the Italians, who had spirited the Duce away from his Roman palace, keeping him? Under normal circumstances it would not have been too difficult to find out his whereabouts. But in July, 1943, the Germans stationed in Rome were treating their erstwhile Italian allies with kid gloves in the vain hope that, in spite of their removal of Mussolini, they were going to honour their pledges to the Axis powers and continue to fight with Germany. As a result Skorzeny could not attempt any of his rough, down-to-earth methods to find the vanished dictator. He was like a blindfolded boxer fighting in the dark.

All he knew was that Mussolini had been arrested during a visit to the King of Italy's palace, bustled into an ambulance and driven off to an unknown destination at top speed. Now, although Rome buzzed with rumours about his whereabouts, Skorzeny was as much in the dark as Himmler, his chief, who had been forced to resort to the services of an astrologer in the hope that he might reveal where Mussolini was being hidden.

Then, after three weeks of futile planning and searching, Skorzeny got his first clue. During this period of frustration

26

Skorzeny and Radl had got to know a fruit dealer, who often visited his customers in Terracino, a little town on the Gulf of Gaeta. Here the fruit dealer's best customer had a serving girl who was engaged to one of the carabinieri stationed on the fortress island of Ponza, to which in earlier days Mussolini had been wont to send his important political prisoners. For the last few weeks the guard had not come on leave to see his beloved. To the fruit dealer and Skorzeny this indicated that Ponza was housing a specially important political prisoner. Was it Mussolini?

A few days later this suspicion was confirmed by the statement of a young Italian naval officer that the Duce had been taken on board his cruiser at La Spezia and brought to the island. Quickly the news was flashed to Hitler's headquarters. Equally quickly the reply came back from the Führer: 'Board the cruiser and free the Duce!'

As Skorzeny was to write after the war: 'This gave us a headache for twenty-four hours. How could you steal someone under the eyes of a whole ship's complement?' But Skorzeny need not have worried. One day later came the news that Mussolini had already been moved from the island. The chase was on again.

After being imprisoned for a short time in a remote village on the island of Sardinia, Il Duce was moved to the fortified port of La Maddalena, on a tiny island some three miles from Sardinia, where he was reported to be imprisoned in a house with the German name of Villa Kern.

Skorzeny wasted no time; Hitler was breathing down his neck to rescue Mussolini. Disguising himself as a German sailor and taking with him a German officer, Lieutenant Warger, who spoke perfect Italian, the German commando leader crossed over to Sardinia, where there was a small German naval detachment with whom they made contact. While Warger started to do a tour of the bars (although he was a teetotaller) Skorzeny took out a motor boat to have a look at the general situation of the coast.

Warger's tour of the bars paid off. Insisting drunkenly that Mussolini had already left the island, he was challenged by the local market gardener who supplied vegetables and fruit to Villa Kern, who maintained that Mussolini was still there. Drunk for the first time in his life, Warger reported his discovery to Skorzeny. The plan could be put into operation.

Learning that the Villa was very heavily defended by both ground troops and flak, Skorzeny decided to fly back to the mainland in his Heinkel 111 to fetch reinforcements in the shape of his waiting SS paratroopers. On Wednesday 18 August, 1943, he set off on his trip. Buried in his thoughts, Skorzeny was suddenly jerked from his reverie by the cry 'Achtung, two planes from behind!' Then one second later: 'English fighters!'

Skorzeny rushed to the nearest machine gun. The pilot dived. To Skorzeny it looked as if the German pilot had dodged the British planes. Then suddenly the port engine cut out and the Heinkel started to dive at four hundred miles an hour. There was no chance of parachuting out. Someone cried hoarsely, 'Hold on', and with a crash the bomber hit the sea. Skorzeny felt his ribs go, then everything went black. He was unconscious. But luck remained on his side. He came round to find that the pilot had managed to inflate the rescue dinghy and that he was able to dive and salvage his precious documents, and after a short time they were rescued by an Italian flak ship detailed to protect Mussolini, the crew of which were fortunately not too curious about the 'German soldiers'. The crew lent them fresh clothing and soon they were landed on Sardinia. Skorzeny had broken three ribs.

But there was no time to consider injuries. He had his ribs strapped and headed for the nearest German unit where he borrowed a car. Two days later he was back with Radl, who had thought him dead, and was told by his adjutant that a message had been received from the Führer indicating that Admiral Canaris, the head of the German Secret Service, now knew where Mussolini was. According to Canaris, whom Skorzeny did not trust, Mussolini was being held on the Island of Elba, once the prison of Napoleon. Skorzeny was furious. He felt that Canaris was deliberately misleading the Leader. Using the good offices of General Student he managed to get an audience with Hitler to tell him of his suspicions about Mussolini's place of imprisonment.

For half an hour Skorzeny spoke to a select audience of leading generals and politicians at the Führer's HQ, trying to convince them that Mussolini was being held at La Maddalena, and in the end he won. Hitler took his hand spontaneously and said: 'I believe you, *Hauptsturmführer* Skorzeny! You are right. I am withdrawing my order to attack Elba with paratroops. Have you a plan for attacking La Maddalena? If you have, would you explain it to me?' Skorzeny took out his pencil, and while some of the most powerful men in Germany leaned over his shoulder, he swiftly detailed his plan, already approved by General Student.

The plan was a typical one for Skorzeny, who as a young duelling student had always attacked the head. On the eve of the operation a German vessel would visit La Maddalena apparently on a courtesy call. At the same time a small fleet of speedy motorboats – *R-Boote*, the Germans called them – would enter the port. After paying their compliments to the Italian port commander they would tie up for the night. The following morning a flotilla of minesweepers containing Skorzeny's SS men and commandos would fringe the island and then suddenly make a dash right into La Maddalena. Under the cover of the guns of the German ships already in the harbour, they would unload their men, who would march openly in formation right up to Villa Kern. It was a bold plan, but Skorzeny reckoned that if he marched his men towards the villa there would be no trouble. The Italian guards would be so awed by the sight that they would think there was no hope of offering resistance.

Hitler approved. They all did. But the Führer had one last word of warning for his commando chief: 'You must understand, *Hauptsturmführer* Skorzeny, that if you fail I may have to disown you, since Italy is still nominally our ally. I should have

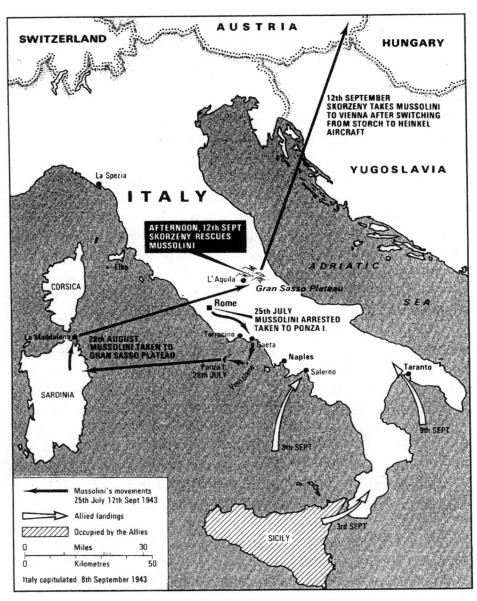

Skorzeny's rescue of Mussolini

Within the map:

AUSTRIA

SWITZERLAND

HUNGARY

12th SEPTEMBER
SKORZENY TAKES MUSSOLINI
TO VIENNA AFTER SWITCHING
FROM STORCH TO HEINKEL
AIRCRAFT

YUGOSLAVIA

La Spezia

ITALY

AFTERNOON, 12th SEPT
SKORZENY RESCUES
MUSSOLINI

ADRIATIC

Elba

CORSICA

L'Aquila
Gran Sasso Plateau

SEA

Rome

25th JULY
MUSSOLINI ARRESTED
TAKEN TO PONZA I.

La Maddalena

28th AUGUST,
MUSSOLINI TAKEN TO
GRAN SASSO PLATEAU

Terracino

Gaeta

Naples

Taranto

Ponza I.
28th JULY

Salerno

9th SEPT

SARDINIA

Ventotene

9th SEPT

3rd SEPT

SICILY

Mussolini's movements
25th July 12th Sept 1943

Allied landings

Occupied by the Allies

0   Miles   30
0   Kilometres   50

Italy capitulated 8th September 1943

to say, for reasons of state, that you acted without orders, that you misled the units supporting you by turning the commanders' heads. Your foolhardy action was prompted by excessive zeal, by ambition even. And if you fail, you must not defend yourself against public repudiation.' Skorzeny nodded that he understood. But when Hitler pressed Skorzeny's hand in parting a little later, he looked up at his gigantic broad-shouldered fellow countryman and said, 'But you will do it, Skorzeny!'

As Skorzeny recalls in his memoirs: 'He sounded so confident that his confidence infected me. I had heard a lot about the hypnotic powers of Adolf Hitler. On this day I had felt them.' (Later when the powers wore off and he told Radl back in Italy of Hitler's threat to renounce them if the mission failed, Radl had said: 'Oh well, we can always share a padded cell in one of Himmler's special sanatoria.')

But the bold attack on the Villa Kern was not to take place after all. A few days later, posing as a sailor, Skorzeny fell in with one of Mussolini's guards who, like Skorzeny himself, was taking a bundle of dirty washing to a laundry near to the Villa which Skorzeny used as an observation post.

Using Warger's knowledge of Italian they fell into conversation with the guard, again suggesting that the Duce was no longer there, that he was in fact dead. At first the Italian would not be drawn, but as soon as Skorzeny mentioned that Mussolini was dead, the guard replied hotly, 'No, no, signor, impossible! I saw him myself this very morning.' He paused for breath, gesticulating with his arms in the Southern Italian manner, and went on, 'That was just before he drove off to the white plane that flew away with him.'

Skorzeny's heart sank. The bird had flown. He would have to start all over again. He cursed himself for not having noticed the absence of the white hospital flying boat in the harbour and the lazy way the guards were now behaving.

Back in Rome, Skorzeny started to search for the missing dictator once again. There were a lot of red herrings and false trails, and time and time again new rumours led him into yet another cul-de-sac. And then he was lucky. While the situation in Rome daily grew more dangerous, with the one German division stationed in the capital surrounded by seven Italian divisions, Skorzeny's Intelligence service intercepted a message from the Rome Ministry of the Interior which read: 'Security measures around Gran Sasso completed.'

It was not much, but the signature underneath the laconic message was significant. It was 'Cueli' and General Cueli was the officer responsible for Mussolini's safety. The clue was sufficient for Skorzeny.

He turned his attention to the Gran Sasso. It was the loftiest peak in the Apennine range of mountains, some one hundred miles from Rome. 6,000 feet up this peak a winter sports centre had been built just before the war, based around the Hotel Campo Imperatore. If the Duce were really being held somewhere on the snowbound mountain, it would be in that hotel, and Skorzeny began trying to find out more about the place. He was lucky. A German resident in Italy who had spent a few weeks there in 1938 gave him some tips. A gaudy leaflet was found which revealed little about the place except that it was connected with the valley below by means of a funicular railway; in fact the funicular was the only way of reaching the hotel. Obviously the place was in an excellent defensive position.

Deciding that Mussolini was being held in the hotel, Skorzeny and Radl squeezed into a reconnaissance plane a few days later and flew over the area, photographing the terrain as they went. Everywhere there were indications that roads leading into the area were heavily guarded and that perhaps a whole division of infantry would be needed to attack the place from the land; and by that time Mussolini might well be dead, murdered by the guards.

When they were directly over the Hotel Campo Imperatore, surrounded on all sides by steep snow-covered crags where it perched on a small plateau, Skorzeny spotted a small green meadow shaped in the form of a triangle just behind the hotel. 'Immediately,' Skorzeny wrote later, 'I decided that that was our landing place.' It seemed to him to be the rifle range that one of his informants had told him was somewhere near the hotel. Satisfied with his day's work the commando chief ordered the pilot to take them back to base.

But again, just as over Sardinia they ran into Allied fighters, this time they encountered American aircraft. Behind them came wave after wave of bombers. Skorzeny did not know it but he was observing the Allied demonstration of power which signalled Italy's exit from the war and the Allied landings at Salerno. Italy had surrendered.

Landing safely at the heavily bombed field (his own quarters had been struck by two heavy bombs), Skorzeny swiftly came to the conclusion that the Mussolini rescue operation would now be a real race with time. Already Italian and German units were fighting, and if Italy's fascists and Mussolini supporters were to be rallied before it was too late, Il Duce had to be freed.

But, as he wrote later, 'a ground operation was hopeless from the start. An attack up the steep, rocky slopes would have cost us heavy losses, apart from giving good notice to the enemy . . . There remained only two alternatives – parachute landings or gliders.'

But the Luftwaffe experts argued that the landing strip behind the hotel was far too small for either, and in any case the air was too rarified for gliders. They estimated that of the hundred men which Skorzeny reckoned he would need to tackle the 200 Italian guards in the hotel, only twenty would survive the drop or glider landing. Nor could Skorzeny budge the Luftwaffe experts.

In the end he ignored them: 'We pondered long on both [alternatives] and then decided in favour of the second. At such altitudes a parachute drop would involve too rapid a rate of descent for anyone equipped with the normal parachute only . . . So a glider landing remained the only solution . . . After this decision had been given, Radl and I worked out the details of our plan. We had to make careful calculations of the distances, make up our minds as to what arms and equipment the men should carry and, above all, prepare a large-scale plan showing the exact landing place for each of the twelve gliders. Each glider could take ten men in addition to the pilot. Each group must know exactly what it had to do. I decided that I would go myself in the third glider so that the immediate assault by my own and the fourth group could be covered by the two groups landed.'

That same night he called his men together and put the plan to them, explaining frankly the dangers involved in this operation which Hitler had ordered personally: 'Honestly, the experts don't give much for our chances,' he told the parachutists of the 1st German Parachute Division and the *Waffen* SS. 'They expect us to lose most of our strength even before the fighting starts. I hope it won't be as bad as all that, but our losses are bound to be high. No one is ordered to take part. Anybody who wants to think twice about coming with us or has a family to worry about can drop out now. He will have nothing to fear. His refusal will not be known outside our ranks nor put into any record and we shall respect him no less.'

Skorzeny paused to let his words sink in. swinging his eyes round the experienced soldiers' faces. Then he said, on an easier note, 'I shall lead the operation myself and I can promise you I'll do my best. If we all stick together, then it must and will succeed. Volunteers, one step forward!'

The entire parade took one step forward smartly. Skorzeny noted: 'It was a real joy to see that not one of the men stayed behind.'

The rest of that night was spent in discussing the morrow. Skorzeny told his officers and men, 'There are some things you can't work out with a slide rule. That's just where our experts may be wrong; and the Italians too. The safer the enemy feel, the better our chances of catching them unawares. Well, we'll soon know.'

4

Attack on the Gran Sasso

The start had been set for dawn, but the gliders which were coming from the Riviera were delayed. At first Skorzeny had cursed at the delay, but he then realized that by the time they got to the Gran Sasso it would be noon; and no one, especially an Italian relaxing after a heavy lunch, in his right senses would expect an attack at that time of the day.

Radl used the delay to drive to Rome and return with General Soletti, who was pro-German. He told the Italian officer that his help was needed for 'an important enterprise' and bustled him into the waiting car. Skorzeny needed the Italian to prevent 'any unnecessary shedding of blood', as he explained to the somewhat startled general when the latter realized what he had allowed himself to be talked into.

The hours passed. It was a beautiful September day, bright and windless, ideal for the operation ahead. Skorzeny passed through the ranks of waiting men distributing baskets of fruit and trying to take their minds off what lay ahead.

Then it was 12.30 and the twelve gliders were drawn up ready for the men to board. In thirty minutes they would be off. But suddenly the high-pitched wail of the air raid siren sounded. Allied bombers came flashing in low over the airfield, and the men scrambled for the shelters. Bombs fell everywhere on the field, but when the all-clear had sounded and the commandos could come from their hiding places, the gliders were seen to be untouched.

They started to embark. Skorzeny ordered the Italian general to follow him into his glider, where Skorzeny took the front seat with Soletti crouched between his legs. He glanced at his watch. It was one o'clock. He gave the signal to take off. The engines of the towing planes began to roar and soon the little armada was airborne, though unknown to Skorzeny two of his leading gliders were lost immediately they entered the cloud bank, which blotted out all sight at 9,000 feet. 'The interior of the glider was most unpleasantly hot and stuffy,' Skorzeny remembered. 'I suddenly noticed that the corporal behind me was being sick and that the general in front had turned as green as his uniform. Flying obviously did not suit him.'

But Skorzeny had other things to worry about besides air sickness. The thick celluloid side-windows of the DFS 230 German glider were difficult to see through and the pilot was flying blind, relying on Skorzeny's knowledge of the route to guide him to the Gran Sasso. Suddenly the pilot of the Henschel light plane which was towing Skorzeny's glider came through on the telephone: 'Flights One and Two no longer ahead of us. Who's to take over the lead now?'

Skorzeny recollects: 'This was bad news. What had happened to them? At that time I did not know that I also had only seven machines instead of nine behind me. Two had fallen foul of a couple of bomb craters at the very start.'

Undismayed, Skorzeny called back: 'We'll take over the lead ourselves'. Pulling out his parachutist's dagger he hacked away at the canvas deck and wall. Cool air rushed in and the Italian general's colour improved.

Down below the commander could now see the peaks of the mountains. They were beginning to approach their target. Skorzeny writes: 'My peephole was enough to let UB get our bearings when the cloud permitted. We had to be very smart in picking up bridges, roads, river bends and other geographical features . . . Even so we had to correct our course from time to time.'

Then he spotted the valley of Aquila below. It was just short of zero hour and they were on target. He also spotted the vehicles of the land force crawling up the winding valley road. They were on time too. 'Helmets on!' he ordered. Then the hotel came into sight. 'Slip the tow-ropes!'

There was a sudden silence as they cut off from their towing machine with its noisy motor and slowly the glider swung round in a wide circle, the pilot and Skorzeny both searching the ground for the triangular meadow he had noted on his reconnaissance flight with Radl. Then he spotted it, but there was a ghastly surprise in store for him. It was certainly triangular, but it was steep, very steep, and littered with boulders! But there was no turning back now. Crying out at the top of his voice: 'Crash landing! . . . As near to the hotel as you can get!' he tensed his body for the crash.

The glider pilot did not hesitate. He tilted the starboard wing' and the glider went steeply down. For a second Skorzeny wondered if the plane could take the terrific strain, but there was little time for speculation. Lieutenant Meyer, the glider pilot, released the parachute brake, and the frail plane jerked forward and lurched down on the meadow. There was a splintering of thin wood, a ripping of canvas, and then one mighty last heave. The glider slewed to a stop.

Swiftly the first man was out, his sub-machine gun held at the ready. Skorzeny let himself fall out sideways immediately afterwards. They were within fifteen yards of the hotel! They were surrounded by jagged rocks which, though doing much damage to the glider, had also acted as a brake. Skorzeny staggered to his feet clutching his weapon.

On a slight rise near the hotel an Italian soldier was staring down at the shattered glider, mouth wide open, obviously wondering where this big bird had suddenly come from. Skorzeny did not give him time to come to any conclusion but rushed past him, his men following. So far not a shot had been fired, and Skorzeny realized that he had been right to tell his men before departure that no one would fire before he did. It looked as if he were achieving complete surprise; a stray shot would have spoiled it.

As they reached the hotel, a shocked sentry stared at them

unbelievingly. '*Mani in alto!*' (Hands up) Skorzeny rapped. Obediently the man raised his hands. Into an open door. An Italian soldier was crouched over a radio set. Skorzeny did not hesitate. A swift well-aimed kick and the chair was sent flying from beneath the man, who fell on the floor. Swiftly the commando leader crashed home the butt of his Schmeisser machine pistol on to the top of the radio. It flew apart. He looked around; the room led to nowhere.

They scrambled rapidly to the door, and running around the corner were faced by a ten-foot-high terrace. Corporal Himmel offered his CO his broad back, and Skorzeny was on it and up over the terrace in an instant. The others followed at the double. For a moment Skorzeny paused and looked at the façade of the hotel, and then he spotted a well-known face and shaven head. Mussolini! Knowing the Duce spoke German, he shouted: 'Away from the window!' The Duce's face disappeared.

In a bunch Skorzeny's men ran into the entrance of the hotel and collided with a stream of Italian soldiers, struggling with their weapons and helmets, trying frantically to get outside. The Germans cut right through them and booted the support from beneath a machine gun set up in the hall.

Skorzeny ignored the Italians. He butted his way through them: they were too close and too intermingled with his own men to allow him to use his machine pistol safely. He ran up the nearest flight of stairs, and at the first turn of the landing saw Mussolini, guarded by two young Italian officers.

Skorzeny hesitated. The two Italians were similarly hesitant. Lieutenant Schwerdt came through the door behind the CO. At the nearest window two faces appeared, surmounted by the brimless German paratroop helmets. His men had shinned up the lightning conductor. The Italian officers realized that they hadn't a chance of fighting it out, and raised their hands in surrender.

The Italians were hustled out and Skorzeny posted Schwerdt as the Duce's new bodyguard. Now dragging in the two men, Holzer and Benz, he stared out at the scene below. Radl, followed by his team, was running towards the hotel, and behind them crawled *Obersturmführer* Menzel, who had broken his ankle during the landing. Some way off the men from Glider No. 5 were also rushing towards the hotel.

Skorzeny leaned out and shouted at the top of his voice: 'Everything's all right! Mount guard everywhere!'

It was only four minutes since they had landed. Now Gliders 6 and 7 came floating in. They landed safely. Then tragedy struck the enterprise. Glider No. 8 must have been caught in a sudden gust of wind, a thermal current perhaps. It trembled violently. Then it plummeted down like a stone, crashing on a ledge and disintegrating. No one clambered out of the wreckage. The whole team of ten men had been severely wounded.

But Skorzeny had no time to think about the tragedy which had spoiled the hitherto successful landing. He realized that without the team from Glider No. 8, he must put an end to any further Italian resistance at once. Bounding to the door he shouted in his bad Italian. 'I want the commander! He must come here at once!' There was some bewildered shouting, then a bareheaded, moustached colonel appeared.

'I ask your immediate surrender,' Skorzeny said in French. 'Mussolini is already in our hands. We hold the building. If you want to avert senseless bloodshed you have sixty seconds to go and reflect.' Skorzeny waited anxiously, watching the terrain for signs of further Italian resistance. But he need not have worried. Before the minute was up, the Italian colonel reappeared, and in both hands he carried a glass of red wine. With a slight bow he proffered the big German commando the token of surrender. 'To the victor,' he said simply.

Skorzeny thanked him and drank the wine; he was thirsty anyway. Outside there was the sound of cheers. Someone had flung a white bedsheet out of an upper window as a sign of capitulation, and the hotel was theirs.

At last Skorzeny had time for Mussolini. The Duce was unshaven and wearing a blue-grey suit that was too big for him, but there was no mistaking the joy in his broad face. Skorzeny clicked to attention. 'Duce,' he proclaimed formally, realizing that this was an historic moment, 'I have been sent by the Leader to set you free.'

Mussolini was equally well aware of the historic importance of the moment, 'I knew my friend Adolf Hitler would not leave me in the lurch,' he said as he embraced Skorzeny.

For a moment or two they chatted. Then Skorzeny excused himself to see to the disarming of the Italian garrison, including the man whose name had first given a clue to the whereabouts of the Duce, General Cueli, who had picked this day to visit his prisoner. After that task was completed, Skorzeny began to consider his next problem – the get-away.

By now both ends of the funicular were in German hands, but Skorzeny dared not risk the roads as an escape route. The Italians down in the valley would be too strong for his small force. The Duce would have to go out by air, the same way as they had come in.

Before the operation started they had worked out three possibilities: German paratroopers would capture the nearby airfield of Aquila and hold it until three planes from Rome arrived to take away the Italian leader. But although the operation was successful and the paratroopers were in control of Aquila, Skorzeny's radio man could not raise Rome now, try as he might.

The second alternative was to land a light plane and take Mussolini away directly from the plateau. It was a risky business and it also failed. During the landing the plane damaged its undercarriage and could not get off again. All that was left was Captain Gerlach's 'Storch' spotter plane which was presently overhead. Gerlach, who had brought him to Rome, was General Student's personal pilot and a very experienced flier, and if anyone could get them off, he could. Skorzeny called Gerlach down, and he immediately made a perfect landing in spite of the terrain, but when he heard that Skorzeny wanted him to take off again with Mussolini, his face paled. To weigh down his plane not only with Mussolini's two hundred pounds, but also with

Skorzeny's two hundred, seemed madness to him. He refused point-blank to do it.

Skorzeny took him to one side, out of the earshot of the men, and firmly told Gerlach that he could not allow the Luftwaffe man to take the responsibility of flying Mussolini out by himself. If anything happened, he, Skorzeny, would have no alternative but to take his pistol and blow his brains out.

In the end Gerlach gave in. Skorzeny gave out a few final orders to Captain Radl and Major Mors, then clambered into the plane behind the pilot. Mussolini, dressed in an overlarge black coat and a broad-brimmed hat, crouched between his legs.

Gerlach switched on the motor and twelve men clung to the little plane, digging their boots into the soil as Gerlach revved up the engine to top pitch. The wind whipped at their hair and blew their camouflaged smocks tightly against their bodies. The noise rose to a crescendo. Still Gerlach did not drop his upraised hand to give the signal to let go. Grimly the twelve commandos held on, the dirt and dust covering them in a grey cloud.

Then Gerlach's hand came down. The men let go: the plane shot forward, and its wheel hit the first rock. It lurched. Desperately Skorzeny flung his weight against the nearest spars to counter-balance the blow. It worked. Mussolini's face went even paler. Skorzeny suddenly remembered that the Duce was also a pilot, and could assess their chances of getting off the plateau only too well. There was another bump. Again Skorzeny flung himself against the steel spars, and again it worked. They rolled bumpily forward, on and on. Would they never take off?

Suddenly a deep gorge loomed up before them. Instinctively Mussolini closed his eyes. But Gerlach had the situation in hand. The Storch shot up and over it, and rumbled on, one wheel badly buckled. And then at last they were airborne. The little plane shot over the edge of the ravine and started a dizzy downwards descent, until with consummate skill Gerlach lifted the Storch's nose up. They had done it.

Behind and below them on the plateau, Captain Radl fainted. It had been a close thing.

A few hours later Benito Mussolini was in Vienna, officially a free man, though unknown to him, he was now entering another, more subtle, kind of captivity.

5
Enter Doctor Wolf

Otto Skorzeny was not unvain. Perhaps it was because he realized the publicity which would be attached to the Mussolini rescue operation that he insisted that he fly out with Captain Gerlach. But even Skorzeny's keen sense of personal dramatization and awareness of the publicity value of the operation he had just carried out gave him little hint of just how much attention it would attract. He had hardly entered the Imperial Hotel in Vienna, where Mussolini went straight to bed exhausted, when the congratulations started pouring in.

Just after Himmler had finished his telephone call, a full colonel entered Skorzeny's room, took off the Knight's Cross of the Iron Cross which he wore around his neck and hung it around Skorzeny's. 'Führer's orders,' he explained. For the very first time the most coveted German decoration was awarded on the same day that it had been won. The colonel was giving Skorzeny his own medal. Hardly had Skorzeny recovered from the surprise when the telephone rang again. It was the Leader.

'Today,' he said joyously from his headquarters in East Prussia, 'you have carried out a mission which will go down in history. You have given me back my old friend Mussolini. I have given you the Knight's Cross and promoted you to *Sturmbannführer* of the Waffen SS.'

Thereafter Göring took over the phone to add his congratulations. He was followed by Field Marshal Keitel. It seemed as if the whole of the General Staff was clamouring to speak with him.

And the festivities, honours, celebrations, award ceremonies and parades did not stop. Göring journeyed to Vienna in his special train to award him the Air Force Medal in Gold (nominally Göring was in charge of the paratroopers). Mussolini gave him the Order of the Hundred Muskeeters. A great rally was held for him at the Sports Palace in Berlin where he pinned medals on the other members of the rescue operation. The *Prominenz* fell over itself to invite the commando into their homes. Ribbentrop, Bormann, Goebbels, Hitler himself – they all requested his company at informal gatherings. Otto Skorzeny was well on the way to becoming a social lion.

And indeed Skorzeny had unwittingly shown the world a new way of conducting the war. What the British had tried and failed to do in 1941 when they had sent a commando group to kidnap or kill General Rommel in the Western Desert, Skorzeny had now successfully pulled off in Italy. Everywhere shrewd military men were realizing that the Viennese ex-engineer had added a new dimension to modern warfare: an extension of armed conflict into the area of such gangster methods as assassination and kidnapping, where one man 'taken care of' in this manner was more effective than the liquidation of a whole army. Winston Churchill was not slow to realize the importance of Skorzeny's rescue of Mussolini in such a daring and dramatic fashion. After giving the House of Commons a full account of the rescue in a speech, he declared: 'The stroke was one of great daring and conducted with a heavy force. It certainly shows there are many possibilities of this kind open in modern war.'

Within the year two young British irregular soldiers would kidnap a German general in Crete and spirit him back to Allied lines in much the same manner that Skorzeny had carried out his operation: a clear indication that Churchill had learned the Skorzeny lesson rapidly and effectively.

But the German commando leader did not like kicking his heels in Berlin as a socialite. He wanted to go back to his men. But before Hitler took leave of his new favourite, he gave Skorzeny the prize he was seeking: special permission to recruit a battalion for every front on which the German army was engaged.

Skorzeny thanked his Leader but was bold enough to enquire where he would get the men from. Jodl told him they would come from the *Brandenburg*, which had now achieved divisional status and with whose men Skorzeny was highly pleased, especially with the aristocratic Captain Adrian von Fölkersam, who spoke French, English and Russian as well as German, and was soon to become his Chief-of-Staff.

Back at Friedenthal, Skorzeny soon found himself deep in new plots. For a while he was sent to France with the task of capturing the French national hero and head of state Marshal Pétain. Pétain and his government in Vichy had long sat on the fence between the Allies and the Germans. Now in 1943 it seemed in the light of Germany's succession of defeats that he might go over to the Allies. It was Skorzeny's job to ensure that he never left France if this happened. But the Pétain mission was called off and the First World War 'Hero of Verdun' lived to stand trial after the war as a traitor.

Hardly had the French crisis been resolved than Skorzeny was rushed to Yugoslavia. Now his orders read 'Get Marshal Tito – dead or alive!' It was a task very much to his liking. The partisan leader had long interested him and he felt he would contribute materially to the success of the war if he could pull off this coup. Also Tito's partisans were keeping thousands of German troops in Yugoslavia when they were urgently needed elsewhere, in particular in Russia.

But the Tito mission was doomed to failure, although Skorzeny risked his life travelling through partisan territory armed only with a sub-machine gun and accompanied by two sergeants. An over-zealous corps commander refused to cooperate with Skorzeny's staff officers and himself launched a full-scale attack on Tito's HQ, complete with parachutists and glider-borne troops as at Gran Sasso. Tito escaped, living to fight another day and to become the respected head of the Yugoslavian state after the war. Disappointed, Skorzeny returned to his HQ for a rest.

But not for long. On 10 September, 1944, he was summoned to the *Wolfsschanze*. After a long tiring day of briefings, he was invited to stay on for the evening's less formal meeting with Hitler. With Keitel, Jodl, Himmler, Ribbentrop and others of the Hitler intimates, he took his place in an easy chair and listened attentively while the Leader delivered a somewhat sarcastic lecture on the situation on the Eastern Front.

Finally Hitler got round to the subject of Germany's major ally in the East, Hungary, 'We have secret information,' he told the group, 'that Hungarian Regent Admiral Horthy is attempting to make contact with the enemy in order to achieve a separate peace for Hungary. That would mean the loss of our armies [in Hungary]. Not only is he trying to negotiate with the Western Allies, he is also trying to arrange talks with Russian leaders.'

There was a shocked gasp of indignation.

Hitler looked directly at his chief commando. 'So, Skorzeny in case the Regent does not honour his pledges, you are to prepare for the military occupation of the Burgberg' (the hill on which Horthy had his residence).

Skorzeny thought of the map he had seen earlier that day on which had been pinned the flags indicating the number of divisions belonging to the Russian army in the Carpathians. If Horthy surrendered, those 120 Soviet divisions would fall among the defenceless, betrayed German troops in the East, one million of them in all. And once the flood tide of the Russian advance had started, perhaps there would be no dam capable of stopping it.

Hitler was still speaking: 'The General Staff has in mind a parachute operation ... you are to start preparing for this operation immediately as the corps staff is currently just being set up. Now in order that you are not to be faced with any difficulties, I am going to give you far-reaching powers.'

Then it was the turn of the 'brains' at Hitler's headquarters: the cunning General Jodl, much more intelligent than the wooden Field-Marshal Keitel, the chief army officer at the *Wolfsschanze*. He sketched in the forces to be made available to

Skorzeny. He was to get a squadron of gliders, two paratroop battalions, and an elite formation made up of hard, battle-experienced, fanatical young officer-cadets. In addition he was to be given a special plane for his own private use from Hitler's special flight.

He was handed a sheet of so-called State-paper bearing the golden eagle of the German Reich, granting him far-reaching powers and signed by Hitler himself, and the Führer wished him goodbye, reminding him significantly: 'And remember, Skorzeny, I'm counting on you.'

Skorzeny forgot his preparations for resistance to the Western Allies who were rapidly approaching the frontiers of the Reich itself: he forgot his concern with the 'vengeance weapons' – the V1s and V2s – which were going to save the day for Germany, once they were available in large numbers. Now he had a task after his own heart. The business with Admiral Horthy might well be the Gran Sasso all over again.

A few days later a certain Dr Wolf from Cologne landed in Budapest, dressed in civilian clothes and with a somewhat dog-eared Baedeker in his hand. Taking up residence in a fairly modest hotel far from those frequented by the German officers stationed in the Hungarian capital, Dr Wolf began to study the environment of the Burgberg (the Castle Hill) in true tourist manner. Dr Wolf, naturally, was Otto Skorzeny. At the same time Skorzeny tried to find out as much as he could about Horthy and his attitudes from his local German sources in the capital. Although their information was often conflicting, all were agreed that the ageing admiral was very much under the influence of his younger son Miklos 'Miki' Horthy. Miki was the *enfant terrible* of the family, notorious for his wild parties and wild life, who nevertheless had been the apple of his father's eye since the older son Istvan, a pilot, had been killed on the Eastern Front in Russia.

Then Skorzeny learned that Miki had already begun to negotiate with representatives of the Yugoslavian partisan chief Tito and had agreed to surrender to the Russians for whom Tito was acting as a middleman. Accordingly he decided to aid the local Gestapo in their plan to capture the young roué the next time he met with the Yugoslavian agents. Operation 'Mickey Mouse' was under way.

On Sunday, 15 October, 1944, the young Horthy agreed to meet the Yugoslavs in the second-floor office of a house in a square near the Danube. Immediately the Germans planned to take over the upper floor of the house and when business had been in progress for about five minutes to burst in on the treacherous meeting while Skorzeny and his men moved in on the conspirators from the outside.

It was a quiet, autumn Sunday morning when Dr Wolf drove up to the square, seemingly empty save for two Hungarian trucks parked outside the building in question. A little further off there was a canvas-backed army truck and a car which Dr Wolf recognized as young Horthy's.

He parked opposite and, opening the hood of his car, pretended to fiddle with the engine. An enquiring hand jerked back the canvas hood of the truck and Skorzeny was able to get a quick glimpse of three soldiers hunched over a machine gun. The Hungarians were prepared for trouble.

But so was Skorzeny. A few moments later two German *Feldgendarmen* – MPs – strolled up. Then suddenly they lost their air of casual unconcern. Before anyone could stop them, they darted into the building. The Hungarians reacted at once. They jerked back the canvas and opened fire. A German policeman fell to the cobbles. Skorzeny dragged him behind the car. Bullets pattered against it like heavy rain on a tin roof. The battle had started.

A number of Hungarian soldiers who had been loitering in a nearby park rushed across the square to join their comrades in the truck. Skorzeny received reinforcements too. His driver got hit in the thigh as he ran across and slid to the ground next to his chief. But Skorzeny wasn't having much luck in the uneven street battle; the Hungarians were armed with a heavy machine gun while his men only had pistols. It was time that Captain von

Fölkersam came to the rescue. Skorzeny blew three sharp blasts on his whistle. The Baltic aristocrat sprang into action, and at the double he and his men pelted up the cobbled street.

The sight of the German reinforcements took the heart out of the Hungarians. They fled from the truck. But not into the conspirators' house. That was good enough for Skorzeny. At the head of his men he ran for it, with his troops throwing 'potato masher' stick-grenades as they ran. The Hungarians retaliated with bricks, marble slabs and heavy pieces of concrete from the roof. But these unusual weapons did not stop the raiders. They penetrated the house to find that the Germans planted up in the top floor had already captured young Horthy and were holding him captive at pistol point. But the favourite son of the Regent was not taking his sudden captivity calmly. He was waving his hands in the air angrily and threatening dire revenge on the Germans when Skorzeny burst into the room.

The big Austrian was in no mood for the young playboy's foolishness. His eye fell upon a large flowered carpet on the floor of the room. Near it a curtain rope – a thick piece of tassel – hung from a window. Swiftly he rapped out an order. Without ceremony young Horthy was flung on the floor. While he struggled in vain, the carpet was wrapped around him. In an instant the bundle was strapped up by means of the curtain rope.

'To the airfield.' Skorzeny commanded, 'I'll follow.'

He paused while Horthy's friend Bornemizza was similarly wrapped in a carpet bundle and carried outside to the truck, then said to Captain von Fölkersam. 'And no more shooting, understand?' The young officer nodded.

The whole action had taken less than ten minutes. Now the question remained: how would the old Admiral take the kidnapping of his favourite son? Would the daring action have the desired effect and keep Horthy in the war on Germany's side?

In the hotel which served as German HQ, Skorzeny waited impatiently for news of the Hungarian reaction. The time passed heavily. A telephone call was received from the German legation that Horthy's residence on the Burgberg was completely sealed off from the outer world; all the roads were barricaded and guarded by heavily armed soldiers. The Hungarians had even laid mines on the key approaches to Horthy's palace.

Then Radio Budapest cut into its normal programmes to announce that the populace should stand by for an important announcement by the Regent. It was two o'clock precisely.

The ageing sailor began his statement with an angry tirade against his erstwhile German ally. The Germans had lost the war, he stated firmly, and Hungary must make a decision. His decision was to make peace with the Russians. He concluded his announcement with the statement that he had already drawn up a provisional armistice with the advancing Red Army. Hostilities between the Russians and Hungarians would cease at once.

The daring kidnapping scheme had failed.

But a disappointed Skorzeny was shaken out of his mood of depression by the news that with typical Hungarian carelessness the Regent had forgotten to notify his armies officially that hostilities had ceased; all they knew was what they had heard on the radio. Accordingly they were showing themselves reluctant to drop their weapons and let the Russians advance through their positions. Perhaps there was still a chance to save the situation?

SS General Bach-Zelewski, a hulking brutal soldier, wanted to destroy the Burgberg by means of a huge 25-inch mortar that had been used to smash into the Black Sea fortress of Sebastopol in the early days of the campaign in Russia. But Skorzeny managed to convince him that such an action would mean the end of any hopes of a German-Hungarian understanding. After some discussion the two SS officers agreed to throw a cordon of the 22nd SS Panzer Division around the Burgberg and wait for a little longer before Operation *Panzerfaust* (the one-shot German bazooka) was set in motion.

Panzerfaust was the plan for the storming of the Castle Hill. Again it would be a typical Skorzeny action. The leisurely movement of the 22nd Division into its position around the hill would indicate to the trapped Hungarians that the Germans intended a long-drawn-out siege of the place or at least that was what Skorzeny hoped. Then at dawn a couple of sorties would be launched against the Hungarians to distract their attention. In the meantime Skorzeny would slip through the Hungarian defences along one of the main roads, his men sitting in their vehicles as if they were on a normal road march – until they were level with the Hungarian positions. Then they would go into action.

The assembled German staff officers shook their heads doubtfully. It was very risky. The sorties to be carried out by the officer-cadets were to be launched against the steep sides of the Burgberg, where the Hungarians were well dug in; they might well suffer heavy losses. Their main objection, however, was to Skorzeny's decision to drive up to the Hungarian positions in his vehicles. If the Hungarians took his defenceless men from the side – one machine gun would suffice – they would be slaughtered. Nevertheless Skorzeny insisted the plan would be carried out in the manner he had suggested.

Some time that same evening a Hungarian general made his appearance at German headquarters. He protested against the appearance of the SS division on the Burgberg. What was the German intention? Were they planning military action against their allies?

The Germans retaliated by asking why their German diplomats were confined to their quarters on the hill; what was the Hungarian intention with them?

The Hungarian flushed with shame and Skorzeny took this as a sign that the man had a conscience and was embarrassed by the recent offer of peace to the Russians. Swiftly he took advantage of the man's embarrassment and suggested that he should have the barriers and mines removed from the Wienerstrasse, which led up to the German Embassy. The Hungarian said he would see what he could do. The time was now two in the morning.

At three Skorzeny took up his position at the head of his men. It was pitch black and he had no idea whether the Hungarians had removed the mines from the Wienerstrasse, the road he had now decided to use for his bold stroke. But he told his officers and NCOs that he wanted no firing unless it was absolutely necessary. Their job was to get through the Hungarian positions without a fight. After all, as he told them, 'the Hungarian soldiers are not our enemies. This must be our motto.'

At five-thirty, as the dawn started to stain the night sky a dirty white, the long column set off. In the front Skorzeny led the group in his army Volkswagen; behind him came four panzers, then a troop of 'Goliath' tanks, a miniature remote-controlled vehicle filled with high explosives, and then truckload after truckload of infantry. Thirty minutes later they were at their start line. There were a few minutes to spare and Skorzeny strolled over to von Fölkersam, who with five old comrades from the Gran Sasso operation, was to form his assault troop. The men were weighed down with machine pistols and stick grenades. They were slightly worried about the reaction of the Hungarian tank troops known to be on the hill, but otherwise confident that they could pull if off.

At one minute to six Skorzeny brought down his arm, as the signal to start. Hurriedly the men clattered back to their vehicles, motors sprang to life and the stillness of the morning air was rudely shattered. The tanks began to clatter forward emitting thick blue diesel fumes from their exhausts. Operation *Panzerfaust* was under way.

Skorzeny licked his dry lips as they began to crawl up the Wienerstrasse that led to the German Embassy. Had the mines been removed? Every moment he expected the explosion which would mean the end of his existence. He tensed himself. Fifty metres ... one hundred ... one hundred and fifty. Nothing happened. The Hungarians had removed the mines!

They were coming up to the Wienertor. Behind him the tanks crawled up the hill at a good twenty miles per hour. Things were going well. Sentries appeared out of the shadows. Skorzeny waved cheerfully. The sentries stood to attention. They had no orders to stop the Germans. Behind him in the tanks the commanders saluted from their open turrets. The Hungarians let them pass. They were through the first obstacle.

Somewhere far off came the crump of explosives. But Skorzeny did not let himself be deflected. They were approaching the German Embassy. and beyond it ran the road to Horthy's palace, straight and not too steep. Skorzeny nudged his driver in the ribs, and he put his foot down hard on the accelerator. The Volkswagen shot forward, and the rest of the column also picked up speed. Half split off to take a second road that also led to Horthy's palace, and the hill echoed with the roar of tanks and military vehicles. Skorzeny knew that the whole Hungarian garrison must be roused by now, that trouble could not be avoided, but still he pressed on.

Suddenly three Hungarian tanks loomed up. When their commanders saw the German attack force, they obviously decided that discretion was the better part of valour. The first one raised his long cannon skywards to indicate that he did not intend to fire, and Skorzeny's jeep sped by them. Suddenly a three-foot-high barrier confronted him. His driver swerved to one side with a squeal of brakes, and Skorzeny signalled to the Tiger behind him. The tank did not hesitate: at full speed it rushed the barrier, and nearly seventy tons of metal crashed into it. The barrier gave and the Tiger rumbled on – to be faced by six manned anti-tank guns!

What would the Tiger commander do? Skorzeny did not wait to see. He was out of his Volkswagen in a flash and through the nearest doorway. Fölkersam's assault group followed. Everywhere the alarm was sounding. A bareheaded Hungarian colonel came rushing out, pistol in hand.

Von Fölkersam knocked it out of his hand, and they rushed on.

Another Hungarian officer came running out of the shadows. 'Lead us to the Commandant of the Burgberg at once!' Skorzeny panted, trying to trick the man.

It worked. Tamely the man ran at Skorzeny's side. giving him directions. They crossed a long section of red carpet, then went

53

up some stairs. The Hungarian officer indicated they should turn right. Skorzeny ordered his men to take up a defensive position while he went on alone.

The Hungarian indicated a door. Skorzeny flung it open. A Hungarian soldier lay on a table pushed up against the open window crouched over a machine gun which was firing into the courtyard below. Skorzeny rapped out a quick order. Sergeant Holzer pushed by him and, grasping the machine gun, he pulled it from the surprised soldier's hand and flung it out of the window. The shocked Hungarian fell off the table and lay helpless on the cartridge-littered floor.

Skorzeny saw another door. Rather surprisingly. he knocked on it, and it was opened by a Hungarian major-general. 'Are you the Commandant of the Burgberg?' he asked. Then, without waiting for him to answer, he said firmly, 'I demand you surrender the Burgberg at once! You are responsible if any more blood is spilled. I ask you for an immediate decision.'

In the moment's silence that followed, he could hear the sound of single shots and the slow irritating chatter of ancient Hungarian machine guns. 'You see,' Skorzeny urged, 'all resistance is foolish. I've already taken the castle.' He guessed that another company of his men under Captain Hunke had already captured most of the key points in the immediate area. As if by telepathy, the next moment the powder-burned Captain appeared and reported, 'Yard and main entrances taken without a fight. Request further instructions.'

The man's appearance had the desired effect. Slowly and nervously the Hungarian said in German, 'I surrender the Burgberg to you and will order the immediate cessation of fire.' Skorzeny and he shook hands and the major-general went on to carry out his decision.

Skorzeny, for his part, moved on to another room which he found filled with antagonistic Hungarian officers. Before they could protest, however, he appointed two of them, both majors, as his liaison officers. They were to take charge of the surrender of their own men: Skorzeny did not want to humiliate the

Hungarians. He still planned, if it were possible, to retain them as Germany's allies and ensure they continue to fight on his country's side.

Then he requested all the officers to come with him into the Coronation Hall where he addressed them in German. It was his first speech in such a setting and to such an audience under these unusual circumstances and he was aware that he owed them and the occasion a suitably solemn and significant speech. His Viennese tongue and charm did not fail him.

'I would like to remind you, he said in German 'that for centuries Hungarians have never fought against Austrians. Always we have been allies. Now there is no reason for difficulties ... our concern is a new Europe. But this can only arise if Germany is saved.'

As Skorzeny remembers: 'My Austrian accent obviously supported and strengthened the effect of my words: something which I felt in the pressure of their hands when I shook hands with each one of them afterwards.

Operation *Panzerfaust* was over at the cost of less than twenty German casualties. Horthy was taken to Germany by a special train 'as a guest of the Leader' and his abdication was announced almost immediately afterwards. He was replaced by Count Szalasi who, being pro-German, at once cancelled the armistice proclamation.

Skorzeny, in the meantime, had taken up residence in the palace, enjoying the life of a 'King in France', as the German expression has it, taking a bath that very evening in the baroque bath-tub once used by the old Austrian-Hungarian Emperor Franz-Josef. It was a just reward, ordered by Hitler himself, for a man who had kept Hungary in the war and saved the whole centre section of the German front in the East. For the remaining nine months of the war the Hungarian army was to fight loyally at the side of its German allies.

6

Operation Greif

On the afternoon of 21 October, 1944. Otto Skorzeny was ordered to report to Hitler's HQ, *die Wolfsschanze*.

Hitler greeted him with a broad smile and, in spite of his enfeebled health, the result of the July bomb attack on his life and over-indulgence in drugs, he managed to give his favourite commando a firm handshake. 'Well done, Skorzeny,' he said. 'Sit down and tell me about this – this Operation Mickey Mouse'.

Skorzeny told his story in detail, only interrupted by occasional laughter from the Leader when he described how he had rolled the protesting young Horthy in the carpet. Then when he was finished, he rose to go.

But the Leader detained him. 'Stay a while,' he said, as his face regained something of its old energy and enthusiasm. 'I am now going to give you the most important job of your life. In December Germany will start a great offensive. It may decide her fate.'

Carried away by his own enthusiasm, he explained how the Allies expected to find a 'stinking corpse' in Germany, but they were in for a surprise. They had won the 'battle of the invasion' only because they had absolute air superiority. But that would all change. For his new offensive in the West he had picked a time when the weather would be in Germany's favour, with overcast skies and fog. In addition, Hitler said, 'We will employ two thousand of the new jet fighters that we have kept in reserve for this offensive.'

In essence his offensive was aimed at preventing the recruitment of a powerful French army and ensuring that the Allied preparations for the attack to the Rhine would be set back for several months; then his attack in the Ardennes would rush through the thinly held area to the Meuse. From here his tanks would drive a wedge between the Anglo-American armies and capture Antwerp, their main supply port on the Continent. And it would take the British a long, long time to replace their army lost in Europe; they were already scraping the barrel for reinforcements. Perhaps, he mused, a delay of the Anglo-American offensive would mean that the Western Allies would fall out with the Russians; there were already indications of a growing tension between the two groups in Greece.

Hitler concluded his explanation of the overall strategic and political intentions of the new offensive in the West with the words: 'I have told you so much so that you will realize that everything has been considered very carefully and has been well worked over . . . Now you and your units will play a very important role in this offensive. As an advance guard you will capture one or more bridges on the River Meuse between Liège and Namur. You will carry out this operation in British or American uniform. The enemy has already used this trick. Only a couple of days ago I received the news that the Americans dressed in German uniform during their operations in Aachen.'

He paused briefly while Skorzeny tried to take in all the new information and remember the geographic details without the aid of notes or a map.

'I know you'll do your best,' Hitler continued. 'But now to the most important thing. Absolute secrecy. Only a few people know of the plan. In order to conceal your preparations from your own troops, tell them that we are expecting a full-scale enemy attack in the area between Cologne and Bonn. Your preparations are intended to be part of the resistance to that attack.'

Skorzeny nodded and then said, 'But the time is short and I have other tasks.'

Hitler didn't answer for a moment, then he replied, 'Yes, I know time is short. But I know you'll do your best. For the

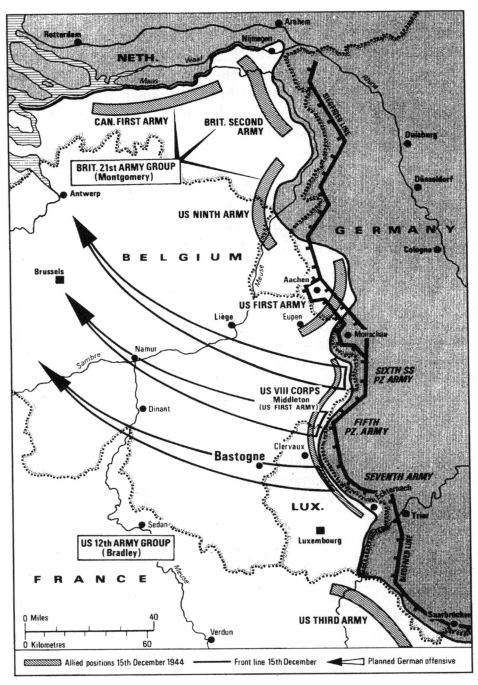

Germany's plan for a counterattack across Belgium

period of the offensive I am sending a deputy. But one thing, Skorzeny, I do not want you to cross the front line personally. You must not run the risk of being captured.'

With that Hitler rose and accompanied him to the door, where he was introduced to General Guderian, the tank expert, and received further orders. Skorzeny had been initiated into Hitler's 'last gamble', the final great land battle of the war in the West, which one day would be named 'The Battle of the Bulge'.

But hardly had Skorzeny set about forming his special troop, which was going to have the title 'Panzer Brigade 150' when he received a circular, which led him to the conclusion that it was no use going on any further with his supposedly 'top secret' Operation *Greif* (Gryphon).

The circular was signed by Field-Marshal Keitel himself and read as follows:

'VERY SECRET: To Divisional and Army Commands Only. Officers and men who speak English are wanted for a special mission. Volunteers who are selected will join a new unit under the command of Lieutenant-Colonel Skorzeny to whose head-quarters at Friedenthal application should be made.'

In particular, Skorzeny was concerned that his Stielau-unit was trained correctly. Captain Stielau was the last of six company commanders who had followed each other in quick succession between 10 November and 16 December, the start of the offensive, a fact which reveals the strain that the commander of this special unit had to undergo.

The Stielau unit was well equipped with captured American weapons, uniforms and vehicles. It consisted of some eighty men, who all spoke from excellent to passable English. It was divided into two groups: the sabotage group in eight jeeps and the reconnaissance group in six. The reconnaissance group was in turn divided into four short-range recce teams and two long-range groups. In each vehicle the crew numbered either three or four men, consisting of driver, radio operator, interpreter and saboteur, who in addition to their normal infantry weapons also carried a phial of prussic acid or cyanide in their army issue cigarette lighters (concealed in the cotton wool) to poison themselves if they were captured.

It was these groups who were to make the initial breakthrough, sabotaging US installations, spreading terror and chaos and penetrating to the vital Meuse bridges.

But already rumours were beginning to spread through the ranks about this elite unit. Some of them thought they were to strike through Belgium into France and then link up with the German garrisons still besieged in the ports of Lorient and Dunkirk. Others thought they were going to be employed to assassinate key British or American generals. One day a young officer who knew Paris intimately sought Skorzeny out in his office. Because of his knowledge, he told Skorzeny that he felt he could be of great use in the forthcoming operation.

'Why?' his CO asked, surprised. 'Because we are going to dash across France through the American Army and capture Eisenhower's headquarters.'

Skorzeny was shocked. 'Where did you hear that?' he asked, and then added: 'Don't mention it to anyone . . . When the time comes I'll call on you.'

The next day the camp was buzzing with the latest hot rumour. They were going to kidnap Eisenhower. The great Eisenhower raid story was born, which was going to plague Eisenhower for a few days at the height of the offensive and Skorzeny for many years to come. For soon, when the first of the Stielau men were captured, they would confess to their captors (as did Corporal Wilhelm Schmidt just before he was executed 'Our unit included a group of engineers, whose job it was to destroy headquarters and kill the headquarters personnel.' Or Peter Ackermann, who was captured as 'Captain Murray Eddie O'Connor' when he stated, 'At the end of ten days no one was in any doubt as to our object. The Officers' Mess waiters passed on everything.'

Working feverishly, Skorzeny ignored the rumours, allowing only a few of his top commanders full insight into the real objectives of his force which he had now divided into three tactical groups, one infantry and two armoured, with a total of seventy German tanks camouflaged to look roughly like Shermans. They would immediately follow into the breach in the American line expected to be made between Recht and St Vith in Belgium, hoping to be taken for members of the US 5th Armored Division which in reality was on the Ninth Army front further north (the attack against the Americans would be launched on the US First Army front). If they were lucky they would be able to fight and trick their way alongside Colonel Peiper's 1st SS Panzer Division's Battle Group, which was to lead the drive of Sepp Dietrich's Sixth SS Panzer Army to the Meuse bridges, till they linked up with the recce teams already hopefully in position near the bridges. By means of such recognition signals as blue lights during the daytime and red ones at night, an unbuttoned second button on the tunic, a particular way of lifting the helmet, particular letters on the left side of the vehicle's hood such as C, D, X, Y and Z, the two groups – Peiper's and Skorzeny's – would be able to identify each other.

It was risky, hurriedly prepared and could well end in death in front of a firing squad for all the men of the Stielau unit (in spite of the German lawyers' briefing that as long as they took off their American uniforms before they fired their weapons they were safe), but still Skorzeny was confident that he could pull it off. He had done it before and he would do it again.

There was only one problem. At his last meeting with Hitler, before the start of the offensive, the Führer told him once again, 'I forbid you categorically to cross the front line, Skorzeny.' Forgetting even to say 'Heil Hitler' in his disappointment, he told von Fölkersam of Hitler's command.

The latter smiled understandingly and said, 'Don't worry, the soup is never eaten as hot as it is cooked', meaning things never work out as they are planned. 'Let us wait and see.'

As Skorzeny recorded later: 'I had an attack of rage. It was clear to me that this order would already be in the hands of the enemy Intelligence people . . . I dictated a "flaming protest" to the Leader's Headquarters with the "obedient" request to have the operation cancelled.'

But his request was turned down by one of Hitler's intimates, the former jockey, Fegelein, an SS officer and soon to be brother-in-law of the Führer. Even Himmler had not the power to change the original plan. When Skorzeny told him of the leakage, he shrugged his shoulders and said, 'Well, it's happened, but the attack must go on.'

With heavy heart, feeling that he was preparing his men for a suicide mission, he started to call in the volunteers, of whom there were many (for Skorzeny's name had an irresistible attraction for the adventurous, bored and dissatisfied). They poured in, not only from the army, but from the navy and the air force as well.

They were in great spirits, fine young experienced soldiers, all of whom clamoured for the chance to take part in this 'suicide mission', as their CO was beginning to call it. But if they were ready for anything in the way of combat, they were certainly not ready for the qualifying test in English. Two thousand men reported for Operation *Greif*, but in most cases their knowledge of the English language was limited to 'yes', 'no' and 'okay'. In the end only a couple of hundred proved to have a satisfactory knowledge of the language and of these only some fifty men really knew English. These were mostly sailors who had served on American ships or men who had lived in the United States and possessed in some cases American nationality. One or two had even served in the US Army.

Skorzeny soldiered on, fighting desperately to get the necessary American equipment and clothing for his force which would eventually number some 3,500 men. Overcoats arrived. They turned out to be British. They were sent back. Six armoured cars were delivered. They too were British, but before Skorzeny could protest they all broke down and proved fit only for scrap. Obviously the British had abandoned them for that reason. For days Skorzeny fought a running battle with higher headquarters before he obtained a supply of captured American field jackets. But slowly, bit by bit, he got his equipment together: a handful of Shermans, fifteen jeeps, several White half-tracks and scout cars. And what he did not have, he made up for by camouflaging German tanks and vehicles with false turrets so that they looked like American armoured vehicles, at least from a distance.

But his problems were still not over. He had to get some sense of organization and purpose into his mixed bag of new recruits. To begin with he isolated them at the German tank training ground of Grafenwohr near Nuremberg. Here they were placed behind barbed wire, as if they were prisoners themselves.

The new recruits had their paybooks taken from them and were forced to drop all their links with the outside world, not being allowed to leave the camp for their whole period of training. Indeed the French historian Jacques Nobecourt states that one man was actually shot 'for having sent home a letter giving too full a description of his existence, in contravention of the oath of complete silence which he had given.' And 'Isolation was so rigorously maintained that the sick were not sent to hospital; as a precaution the others were dosed against influenza and colds.'

One man remembers his time in the camp as follows: 'A group of armed sentries made it quite clear that we had lost our freedom now that we had entered the camp. My bunk was in the block occupied by Captain Stielau's group. Almost immediately I was struck by the unusual almost unsoldierly attitude of the members of this unit. In an astonishingly short time, we achieved a feeling of "togetherness", which you usually find only among soldiers in times of great stress at the front . . . At first we were mostly concerned with learning the idiom of the GIs. The performance of American films, especially war films, played a great role in our training. Then came the day we were sent to American POW camps where we mixed with the GIs and gained the impression that we were developing into perfect Yankees.'

Swiftly, working against time, Skorzeny knocked his special unit into shape. As he saw it, it was not his job to turn these men into special troops, guerrillas or the like. They were all trained, battle-experienced soldiers anyway. What he wanted from them was that they changed their complete pattern of habits.

As he saw it, nationality was a matter of basic instincts, which expressed themselves in certain habits and attitudes. These he had to change. Not only did his men have to learn how to chew gum, they would also have to learn to relax on street corners, take things casually, loosening up bodily as GIs did. It was no use dressing a man in olive green and giving him gum to chew and then have him spring to attention rigidly like an old-time Prussian as soon as an officer gave an order. The pseudo-GI would be discovered at once.

7

The Most Dangerous
Man in Europe

Precisely at 0530 hours on the morning of 16 December, 1944, 2,000 German guns of all calibres crashed into noisy action all along the eighty-mile Belgian Ardennes front. Exactly one minute later the first 14-inch shells started to land in the area of St Vith. The first frightening salvo struck down on the border town and awoke the terrified Belgian civilians and their American liberators to the fact that the Germans were coming back.

An eruption of flame and smoke burst all along the front which the GIs sent there to rest or acquire front experience called the 'Ghost Front'. The ground shook with the impact of falling shells. For one hellish half hour it continued. Then as abruptly as it had started it stopped. There was silence. The civilians began to crawl out of their shelters and the soldiers to pop their heads over the tops of their foxholes. What was going on? What was this about?

They were soon to find out.

At 0600 hours, the first white-clad infantry commenced their assault on the border villages held by the Americans of the 14th Cavalry Group on the 2,000-yard sector of the front that linked the positions of the 99th US Infantry and 106th Infantry Divisions, both highly inexperienced formations. The Americans crumbled. One after another the six fortified villages were taken. But the American resistance was stiffer than the Germans on the Sixth SS Panzer Army front had expected. The attack division, the 3rd Parachute, was only a little less inexperienced than the American formations which it was attacking. It was taking too much time to clear the *Amis* away and there were too many casualties.

Behind the parachute infantry the elite armoured formations of the Sixth SS Panzer Army began to pile up. A fuming *Obersturmbannführer* Peiper, thirty-one years of age and, like Skorzeny, a Knight's Cross holder and a Hitler favourite, barrelled his way through his own infantry and enemy minefields to get to the front. Behind him an impatient Skorzeny tried to do the same without success.

As early as 0700 he felt that things were going wrong. Apparently Sepp Dietrich's artillery bombardment had not been as effective as anticipated. The Americans were still holding out, in particular around Losheim. The attack was progressing slowly. By noon reports started to come in at his Schmittheim HQ that there was violent fighting at the front, but little progress. 'The intended collapse of the whole front,' he wrote later, 'had not been achieved.'

Losing patience with the slow progress of the assault infantry, he drove to Losheim himself in order to get a clearer picture of the situation at the front. The road was chaotic, jammed with vehicles of all kinds. Senior officers were out on the street walking or trying to regulate the traffic. In the end he could not get any further with his Volkswagen and was forced to walk nine kilometres to his destination.

He knew now that there was trouble ahead for Operation *Greif*. The success of his adventurous plan depended upon a clean breakthrough on the first day. This was obviously not going to be the case. The natural thing now was to cancel Operation *Greif*. But dare he, after Hitler himself had ordered the operation? And had he not put a lot of work into the bold plan? But then he thought of Peiper, who was as bold and daring as himself. Peiper was scheduled to be thrown in at midnight with his 5,000-man-strong battle group of the 1st SS, one of the best formations in the German army. Perhaps the thirty-one year old SS colonel with his reputation for unorthodox leadership and bravery in action might achieve a breakthrough. He decided to give himself another twenty-four hours before he made his decision to call off the operation.

He spent the rest of the day talking to his remaining recce teams, made up of English-speaking marines who were in high spirits and confident. Then he talked to a few of the first prisoners, who encouraged him by telling him that the offensive had caught them completely off their guard. Thereafter he stole a few hours' sleep in hopes that the new day would bring the good news from Peiper that the latter had broken through and he could start his operation. He fell asleep wondering what had happened to his jeep teams, which had already crossed the line the previous evening.

While Skorzeny slept Captain Stielau's men were already at work, seven jeeploads of them having penetrated the US lines and begun their havoc. The leader of one team had succeeded in directing a whole 3,000-strong American regiment down the wrong road while his men had been tearing up signposts and cutting telephone wires. Another team stopped by an armoured column, simulated terror so convincingly that the American tanks turned round and fled. A further four-man group succeeded in cutting the main cable linking Bradley's HQ in Luxemburg and Hodges, the commander of US First Army, in Spa.

But the greatest damage was done by the capture of the group at Aywaille, south of Liège, some twelve miles from the vital bridge across the Meuse at Engis. An MP asked them for a password and when the three men in the jeep dressed in US uniform did not know it, they were arrested. On them were found German army paybooks, 900 US dollars, 1,000 pounds sterling, two Sten machine pistols, two Colts, one German pistol and six US grenades. Under interrogation they revealed they were members of Otto Skorzeny's long-range penetration group, passing under the names of Charles W. Lawrence, George Sensenbach and Clarence van der Wert. In reality they were Officer-Cadet Gunther Billing, Corporal Wilhelm Schmidt and Lance-Corporal Manfred Pernass.

A few hours later a group of 'American soldiers' appeared out of the forest near the village of Poteau riding self-propelled guns abandoned by E Troop of the 18th Cavalry Squadron which had given up its positions in the Losheim Gap. They passed a sergeant of the 32nd Squadron who thought the GIs' boots looked 'funny'. Before he could challenge them, one of them cried, 'We are E Company'.

That was enough for the suspicious sergeant. In the cavalry there were; no companies, only 'squadrons' or in this case 'troops'.

But not all the teams were captured or killed. At least three returned intact. One had reached Huy, the second had succeeded in crossing the Meuse near the Amay, the only unit of the whole 250,000 strong offensive army to do so, and the third had patrolled in the Vielsalm area. A further two made it back to the Malmédy area with several wounded. This in spite of an American regulation completely unknown to Skorzeny that army instructions forbade the presence of more than three people in one jeep.

But killed, captured or escaped, the effect of those eighty men belonging to Captain Stielau's unit was tremendous. Although there were simply not enough of them to have carried out all the acts of sabotage attributed later to them, they were made responsible for every misled convoy. An enormous anti-sabotage action started behind the Allied lines and spy fear swept through France and Belgium.

'Radio Calais', the Allied propaganda station run by Sefton Delmer, the British journalist, and aimed at undermining the fighting spirit of the German army, reported that some 250 men in American uniform had been captured. And Skorzeny, who received the report, laughed, for he knew that if the number was correct then the Allies must have arrested some of their own soldiers: years later as an Allied prisoner he was to meet some of those men mistakingly arrested. One American captain was arrested because he was wearing a pair of German jackboots. Another two men were put in jail because they remarked while visiting a strange mess that the food was good. Obviously that was a very suspicious remark indeed to make about the products of the GI cooks.

General Bruce Clarke, the defender of the besieged key road- and railhead town of St Vith, was imprisoned by his own men for five hours. Thrust into his own guardroom, the furious General was told by a grinning MP, 'Don't make me laugh. You're one of them Nazi killers.' And no amount of pleading, bullying or reasoning could make them let him go. When they finally did so, one of them had the nerve to ask the general, 'May I have your autograph, general?' Though fuming with rage, Clarke gave him it.

The word went out to look for the 'most dangerous man in Europe', who had sworn to get Bradley, Montgomery and naturally Eisenhower. Soon half the army appeared to be looking for saboteurs and spies. General Bradley, for instance, commenting sourly that 'half a million GIs [were] playing cat and mouse with each other every time they met', soon ran into trouble himself. Attempting to visit General Hodges, he was told by his staff he must wait for a plane because 'the rear areas were being panicked by disguised Germans.' When he overrode their protests and took the road with his car, well decorated with his three stars, he found that 'neither rank, nor credentials, nor protests' spared him being stopped at every road block. Here he had to prove his identity time and time again, 'the first time by identifying Springfield as the capital of Massachusetts (my questioner held out for Chicago); the second time by locating the football guard between the centre and tackle on a line scrimmage; the third time by naming the current spouse of a blonde called Betty Grable.' It was Harry James.

Montgomery took advantage of the situation. He saw an opportunity to get himself a new status. Declaring to Simpson that he was uneasy about the reactions of the trigger-happy GIs who were asking him all sorts of questions he could not answer, he asked the Commander of the US Ninth Army for an American Identity Card. Formal orders came from Washington not to give him it. But he got the treasured ID card all the same.

But the panic-stricken rumours about the Skorzeny men which swept through the American lines had their greatest effect in the headquarters of the Supreme Commander himself. Four days after the offensive had started Eisenhower heard that there was a plot to kill him by a suicide squad of Germans. 'A very agitated colonel,' he wrote in his memoirs, '. . . was certain that he had complete and positive proof of the existence of such a plot. He outlined it in great detail and his conclusions were supported by other members of the Security Staff.'

The result was that Eisenhower had to give up his little villa some distance away from the Supreme Headquarters in the Petit Trianon. It had once been Field-Marshal Rundstedt's HQ and the SHAEF security men reasoned that the Germans would know every inch of the building. It was too risky. He was brought to the Versailles headquarters and kept a virtual prisoner for the next few days.

Perhaps the best description of the atmosphere at Supreme Headquarters during those anxious days is given by his secretary, ex-model Kay Summersby, who wrote in *Eisenhower Was My Boss*: 'Security officers immediately turned headquarters compound into a virtual fortress. Barbed wire appeared. Several tanks moved in. The normal guard was doubled, trebled, quadrupled. The pass system became a strict matter of life and death instead of the old formality. The sound of a car exhaust was enough to halt work in every office, to start a flurry of telephone calls to our office, to inquire if the boss was all right. The atmosphere was worse than that of a combat headquarters up at the front, where everyone knew how to take such a situation in their stride.'

When Eisenhower left to visit another office he was accompanied by what appeared to him to be a whole company of MPs. He was asked in the end not to go outside in case a German sniper managed to sneak into the compound and take his life.

Then security reported that the Germans were massing at the Café de la Paix. The attack would come soon. It was all too much for Eisenhower.

He simply walked out of his office, mumbling to Kay Summersby, 'Hell's fire, I'm going for a walk. If anyone wants to shoot me, he can go right ahead, I've got to get out!'

But for nearly four days Eisenhower was virtually a prisoner in his own HQ at the most critical phase of the sudden German counter offensive. The Skorzeny plan had paid handsome dividends.

While Eisenhower was detained within the Versailles compound for most of the Christmas week, his security men, unknown to the Supreme Commander, were using a human decoy to trap the 'most dangerous man in Europe'. A Lieutenant-Colonel Baldwin B. Smith had volunteered to drive twice daily back and forth between the Eisenhower villa at St Germain and Versailles. The colonel looked somewhat like 'Ike' and had noted one or two of his habits including his particular way of saluting. Accordingly the security men thought the 'Skorzeny killers' might take a crack at him with a grenade or rifle; then they'd pounce on them. Naturally they never did and Lieutenant-Colonel Baldwin Smith was spared for another day.

It is reported, however, that General Eisenhower 'blew his top' when he heard of the use of the human decoy. The deception was never repeated even towards the end of the war when 'werewolves' from the Nazi underground movement were reported to be out to get senior commanders.

But what of Otto Skorzeny himself? On the second day of the offensive he realized that there was little chance of his original operation having any success. The breakthrough anticipated on his section of the front had not been achieved. Peiper had got as far as La Gleize, some twenty miles deep into Belgium, but his drive had been stopped and he was now surrounded. Now the only approach into Belgium for Sixth SS Panzer Army was a narrow bottleneck hemmed in on one side by the stubborn defence of St Vith and on the other by that of the Elsenborn Ridge.

On 18 December Skorzeny made his decision. He requested Sepp Dietrich, Commander of Sixth SS Army, to free him of his

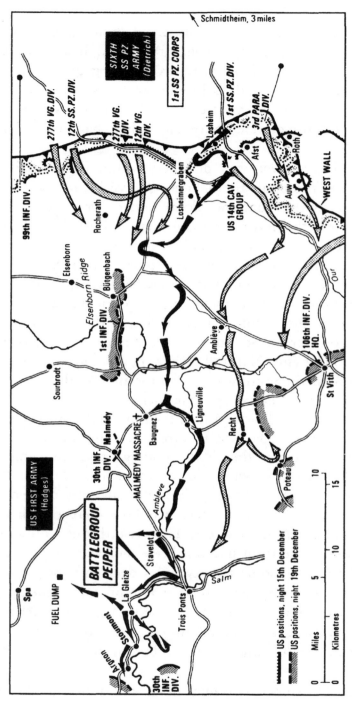

The failure of Operation Greif

original mission and allow him to use his 150th Panzer Brigade for normal purposes, perhaps as infantry because of the brigade's acute lack of armour.

Dietrich agreed and he was attached to 1st SS Corps, which was now understrength because of Peiper's group being cut off from its parent organization. Skorzeny quickly adapted to his new role. He asked SS General Preiss for a mission and was told that he was to take care of the northern flank of the corps, especially, around the road junction at Malmédy which was particularly sensitive to an enemy attack. Skorzeny set up his headquarters in a little farmhouse at the village of Ligneuville and set about preparing an infantry attack on the town of Malmédy itself which was in American hands. After receiving information from one of his teams that the town was only weakly occupied, he decided to attack on the morning of 21 December, coming in from both sides, hoping to take Malmédy by surprise. (The town must really have been weakly held – the Americans bombed it themselves three times with tragic results, apparently believing there were no American troops left there. No figures have ever been revealed on the loss of life during these bombings which the US Air Force denied to the end, but local estimates indicate some 300 civilians and perhaps the same number of GIs were killed. After the bombings Ninth Air Force which carried them out became known as the 'American Luftwaffe' among the men of the 30th US Infantry Division which took the brunt of their attacks.

The two groups went in at dawn, but they met failure. Both Fölkersam and the commander of the other group were hit and wounded, the former in his backside which later caused some amusement when he returned to Skorzeny's HQ. The Americans of the 80th Infantry Division, which had already gained the nickname of 'Roosevelt's Butchers' on the German radio, stopped them dead by the use of the new POSIT proximity fuse. In spite of stubborn resistance here and there by small groups of Skorzeny's men, the rest broke and started to stream back the way they had come. Skorzeny, who dared not go too close to the front because of Hitler's order, stared despondently at the stragglers, knowing that they no longer had the spirit for a second attack. In the end he called it off. Malmédy remained American.

Later that evening, while he was walking over to the divisional CP of the division to which he was attached, located in the internationally famous Hotel du Moulin, he heard the sound of heavy artillery.

Monsieur Peter Rupp, the seventy-year-old owner of the Hotel, saw how the big man staggered and seemed to fall as the fist-sized pieces of shrapnel hissed through the air. He had been hit in the face and blood was pouring down his cheek. A soldier ran out to help him, but Skorzeny waved him away, staggered into the hotel and seized a glass of cognac (left from the supplies of US General Timberlake whose HQ the hotel had been until four days before).

Downing it in one gulp, Skorzeny asked for a mirror to look at his face. As he recorded his feelings at that moment in his memoirs: 'I felt how the blood ran warmly down my cheek. Carefully I felt my face with my hand. Above my eye a lump of flesh was missing from my forehead and was hanging down over the eye. I was shocked. Was my eye gone?' Fortunately it was not.

Some time later Skorzeny allowed himself to be attended to by his regimental doctor, refusing any kind of narcotics save alcohol because he wanted to keep a clear head. The doctor probed with his instruments while Skorzeny bit his teeth, thinking of the old days when he had been a duelling student and had received similar treatment, but the wound proved clean and the doctor could sew it up.

Skorzeny's part in the Ardennes Offensive was over. On the 28th his brigade was relieved by an infantry division and the survivors broken up a little while later. Skorzeny was called to Hitler's HQ three days later to make a personal report.

When the Führer saw Skorzeny's bandaged head, he ordered him to report immediately to his own surgeon, Dr Stumpfecker, who was shocked when he saw the state of the eye. He told Skorzeny he might lose his eye and that he should have gone to hospital immediately after he had been wounded. After this lecture he gave him a series of injections and then re-dressed the wound.

That same afternoon Skorzeny was admitted to the Leader's presence. Surprisingly enough Hitler was full of confidence and enthusiasm. 'We are now going to start a great offensive in the southeast,' he told Skorzeny, and then explained that when it was successful the real Ardennes offensive would be resumed.

Skorzeny left the conference room puzzled, though more cheerful than when he had entered. Where did Hitler get his high spirits from, he asked himself. Was it the result of Professor Morell's injections which he had heard about?

Early that day Dr Rudolf Brandt, another of Hitler's doctors, had told him that Morell's injections and pills contained dangerous substances. 'I recently analyzed one of those stomach pills,' said Dr Brandt. 'It contained arsenic. I warned the Führer, but he wouldn't listen.'

The doctor's statement confirmed Skorzeny in his belief that Hitler was not aware of the true situation in which Germany found itself. As he wrote himself later: 'It was clear to me and my staff officers at the beginning of 1945 that the last phase of the war had begun.' Soon the fate of Germany would be decided in the great battles to come in the East.

The full realization of what was to follow came when he returned to Friedenthal at the beginning of January. Fölkersam was waiting for him. Now that the 150th Brigade was being broken up, he wanted a new assignment. Skorzeny asked him what that might be. Fölkersam knew that there would be no future missions of the kind carried out in Italy and Hungary. Those glorious days were over. He wanted a regular front line assignment. He asked for and received command of the Eastern Skorzeny Group.

Skorzeny never saw him again.

Now Skorzeny began to see another side of the medal. The

carefully planned missions of the old days, carried out by a few brave specialists which usually ended in success, were now replaced by rapidly flung together jobs carried out by bold yet untrained men, whose lives were sacrificed with careless abandon. Now the war began to take on a nightmarish aspect.

There was the case of Lieutenant-Colonel Scherhorn, for instance, who had been cut off in Russia for months, still fighting with the survivors of his 2,000-strong regiment when there were no German troops within a hundred miles of him. Now in January, 1945, six months after Scherhorn had been cut off and three months after Skorzeny had tried to get a Russo-German team to him by parachute with supplies and information, Skorzeny found the High Command was cutting down the fuel supplies needed for the planes which kept the trapped men supplied with food and weapons. One month later when Skorzeny himself was back at the front in a strictly infantry role, he heard that Scherhorn had reached the lakes 200 miles north of Minsk, where German planes could land and take him and his men off to return them to Germany. Thereafter silence.

But in February, 1945, Skorzeny had little time to worry about the fate of Fölkersam or Scherhorn, whose last signal had been: 'Where are the planes? Send to fetch us. Hurry. We are running out of food.' In that month he too was engaged in his own last great desperate battle, the fight to defend the last major water barrier against the Russians in the East, the River Oder, which Berlin Radio described realistically enough in the following terms: 'The last great battle has begun. Enormous masses of troops, tanks and aircraft are being hurled against us in the East. The Russians are out for the final decisions.'

8

Battle on the Oder

For almost two years Otto Skorzeny had not served as a conventional soldier. His sphere of activity had been exclusively that of the irregular. Now, however, in the last months of the dying Reich, he found himself relegated (as he regarded it) to conventional warfare.

On the evening of 30 January, 1945, he was sitting in his office at Friedenthal occupied with some routine office work when the phone rang. It was Heinrich Himmler, the head of the SS, who had now been given command of the *Ersatzarmee* (Reserve Army) in Germany itself, as well as the long sought-after front command – Army Group Vistula.

In actual fact the front was less than two hours away from the German capital itself and Himmler, the frontline commander, had his own 'command post' in the outskirts of Berlin.

Himmler's order was clear and to the point, a sign that the *Reichsführer* was worried, for normally he was not precise, preferring to live (as one of his SS Generals put it cynically) 'with his two feet planted firmly three yards above the ground'. It stated that Skorzeny should march immediately to the River Oder with all available forces and establish a bridgehead east of the river: 'this must be large enough to allow it to be used as the starting point for a later offensive. During the advance to the bridgehead the troops must retake the little town of Freienwalde occupied by the Russians.' Skorzeny knew that Himmler had promised Hitler he would save Berlin from the Russian forces already marching on it. The Oder bridgehead was obviously going to be used by the SS Chief as the starting point for his great two-corps counter-offensive with which he would drive the Russians back. Cynically Skorzeny laughed as he put down the phone. The two corps simply did not exist, except in Himmler's imagination.

Thereafter, while Skorzeny struggled to get his force on the road, the phone from Himmler's HQ never stopped ringing. 'Have you started yet . . . we've already reported to Hitler that you're on your way . . . Why have you not left yet?' The calls went on and on as a desperate Skorzeny not only tried to get together sufficient transport for his motley force, which consisted of an SS parachute battalion and four companies of special troops recruited from a dozen European countries, (even from neutral Sweden), but also to find out information about his target.

It was impossible. No one knew anything about Freienwalde. Neither Himmler's nor Hitler's headquarters knew the position of the advancing Russians. In the end Skorzeny decided simply to march to Schwedt and establish his bridgehead there. Thus it was the next morning at five, he and his 1,000-odd men were ready to march. Sitting in his captured jeep which he had brought back from the Ardennes with Lux, his faithful Alsatian dog at his side, Skorzeny gave the signal to start. The column started to roll. Once again the commando leader was off to the wars.

Two hours later he was on the fringe of the mediaeval town of Schwedt. Above the castle in the centre of the sleepy little town the German flag was still flying. It was still in German hands. Speedily Skorzeny drove to its centre, sending patrols down to the frozen river, while he looked for a site for a command post.

He found a suitable place and set to work at once. His first task was to stop the rot which was only too obvious on all sides. Everywhere pathetic columns of defeated ragged German soldiers straggled westwards, their eyes round with fear or dull and apathetic with defeat. Nothing and no one seemed able to stop them. They were running away.

He rapped out a few orders. A cordon was formed to the west of the town with NCOs manning every exit road. Their job was to stop the retreating soldiers, re-arm them if necessary and then form them into new companies. If he was to defend a bridgehead against the whole weight of the Red Army, he would need all the men he could get.

While this was going on, Skorzeny considered exactly what men were available to him. He had naturally his own well-trained, reliable Friedenthal formations, but they were not sufficient to stop the Russians. What else was at his disposal?

There were the troops still in Schwedt. They consisted of the sick and wounded still in the local hospitals; a handful of engineers who could use a rifle; and one *Volkssturm* battalion, the local home guard, some six hundred strong, made up of very young or very old men, all virtually untrained. Of the local forces the best unit was a 180-strong officer-cadet training group, all seasoned battle-experienced soldiers, who happened to be on a course in Schwedt. They, he told himself when he discovered their presence, would form the nucleus of his new units. Speedily his plans to collect stragglers, regardless of their parent units, started to pay off. The local barracks started to fill up with men of all arms of the service, including cavalry.

One day after Skorzeny arrived in the town, he was astonished to see some twenty-five men on tired old nags come trooping through the main street. At their head a young officer became aware of the high-ranking spectator. He jerked his reins and managed to urge his mount into a semblance of a trot. Halting in front of Skorzeny, he pulled himself to attention and announced 'The remnants of my troop of the Eighth Cavalry, sir! Have you a task for us?'

Skorzeny smiled. Hadn't he just!

'Report to my people at the barracks,' he told the aristocratic young cavalryman, who had a well-known military name. 'Have a good sleep and then report to me again tomorrow morning.'

So they came in, bit by bit, until soon he had the equivalent of four infantry battalions refitting and reorganizing in the local barracks, and he could get down to defending the town and holding the bridgehead.

His first task was to conscript the local population, men, women and children, for the task of digging trenches. Some sharp words to the local party bosses and they let their townsfolk out to carry out the unenviable task in the bitterly cold weather with the ground frozen solid. Then he had a look again at the River Oder. Himmler had regarded it as a natural barrier. But now it was frozen solid, solid enough to bear infantry and light vehicles, perhaps even tanks. He gave orders to use dynamite to blow up the ice. The water started to flow again.

While aggressive patrols penetrated deep into the no-man's-land on the other side of the river, trying to make contact with the advancing Russians to assess their strength, dispositions and intentions, Skorzeny cast around for heavier weapons to arm his men and give them stronger support when the Russians attacked than the present small arms available to them. He commandeered a number of 75mm anti-tank guns from a factory thirty miles away and followed that somewhat high-handed act by obtaining, under similar circumstances, a large number of special machine guns which were going to come in highly useful. Still not satisfied, he rounded up all available 88mm anti-aircraft guns in the area and mounted them on trucks for use as his mobile artillery reserve. Meanwhile more troops were pouring into the area. They weren't the best, but they were better than nothing, he told himself, and, stiffened by his veteran Friedenthalers, they would hold.

While he was thus collecting his forces and their weapons, Göring telephoned. For some reason he was interested in the Schwedt bridgehead, perhaps because he remembered Skorzeny from Vienna after he had awarded him the medal for the Mussolini rescue operation. At all events he displayed considerable interest in the bridgehead as long as it was under Skorzeny's command, actually coming to the front himself one day. Now the excessively fat Marshal inquired, 'How's it going?'

'I could do with some more troops,' Skorzeny answered.

Göring took a note of the other man's wishes and the next day a 600-strong battalion of the Hermann Göring Division arrived from Göring's country home, Karinhall, which lay west of Schwedt. They were fine young men, recruited mostly from air force flying crews who no longer had planes to fly, but they were terribly inexperienced. When Skorzeny saw them he realized they would not last long as an infantry battalion as they had hardly any infantry training. In spite of the protests of their commander, a young major wearing the Knight's Cross of the Iron Cross for bravery, like himself, he broke them up and spread them among his units.

Now he was ready for the Russians. His motley army had reached divisional strength. In all he had some 15,000 men under his command, recruited from virtually every European country, including Russia. Officially the group received the title 'Division Schwedt', but to Skorzeny it seemed the first 'European Division'. As he wrote later: 'In the ranks of the Friedenthal battalions, Norwegians, Danes, Dutchmen, Belgians and Frenchmen fought side by side. One could nearly say that here a European Division was fighting bravely and true. It was a united Europe in miniature.' But Otto Skorzeny was too much of a realist to believe in the effectiveness of the 'One Europe' united in the 'fight against the Reds' which was the last desperate lie spread by Goebbels' Propaganda Ministry in Berlin aimed at rallying as many gullible young men as could be found from all over Europe to the German cause in this moment of decision. It was too late for all that now. This was Germany's battle, and if Europe was united, then it was against the Reich and not with it.

In early February Skorzeny set off with a small patrol to see if he could find the Russians himself. They had just approached the small town of Bad Schönfliess when they came under fire. Almost at once two of his men flopped in the snow, dead. The patrol moved back. But Skorzeny did not give up so easily. He had to ascertain the Russian strength.

At dusk on that same day, he and a handful of other men went out again, approaching the town from a different direction. It seemed deserted. Then they found three civilians lying dead in the road, one a woman. Still no sign of life. Then Skorzeny spotted a pale face peering out of the side of a shattered window – a civilian, and German too.

Wildly excited to see the German troops again, the man raced downstairs to explain breathlessly that the Russians had been in the town for two days. Asked by Skorzeny where they were, he pointed to the station. They had their HQ there, the man said, and tanks as well. They had got the railway going again and were delivering troops and vehicles there regularly.

While Skorzeny crept carefully into the town at the head of a three-man patrol (he found only apathetic women and children left there) his other patrols penetrated as far as the station. There, they reported, they had seen some thirty Russian tanks, mostly T-34s but with some 'LeaseLend' Shermans hidden behind the station as well. The Russians were billeted in houses and camps to the south and east of the town. However, the patrol had not ascertained the Russians' strength. But Skorzeny had enough information for the time being. He knew the enemy's approximate strength and where one of his main railheads was; that sufficed.

It was time to get back. As they stole away, they could hear Russian tanks being started up somewhere over by the station, but by then they had already reached the cover of the thick snow-heavy woods.

It was not long afterwards that the Russians struck. Nearly forty T-34s and what appeared to be several battalions of infantry drove into the city of Königsberg. Fighting grudgingly from house to house, Skorzeny's SS paratroopers retreated, destroying a dozen tanks with the aid of the *Volkssturm* outfit from Hamburg as they went.

But Skorzeny had not only the Russians to contend with. There were enemies enough in his own camp. Returning to Schwedt that same evening, he found the commander of the Königsberg *Volkssturm* waiting for him at his command post.

'*Herr Obersturmbannführer,*' he reported nervously, 'I've been waiting for you all evening. All is lost in Königsberg.'

Although the commander of the *Volkssturm* was a high party official with excellent connections in Berlin, Skorzeny did not hesitate. 'He had simply run away from his unit,' Skorzeny recorded later, 'and had left his men to fight on alone. In the soldiers' language that meant he was guilty of cowardice in face of the enemy and a deserter to boot.' He had the man arrested in spite of the fact he knew he would have trouble with the Party for doing so. (He was right. The chief secretary Martin Bormann swore revenge on Skorzeny for his 'irresponsible action'). Trouble with the Party was not his only problem on the 'home front'. A few days later he learned that the new corps commander on his sector of the front was to be SS General Bach-Zelewski, the 'victor of Warsaw' who had put down the National Polish Uprising in the Polish capital a few months before with great brutality, the officer with whom Skorzeny had already had trouble in Budapest in October. As he anticipated, the general soon started interfering with his command. A flood of orders, requests and demands started to come into his headquarters in Schwedt. Skorzeny raged. As he wrote later: 'What made me angry was that none of his staff officers ever visited the bridgehead. Bach-Zelewski visited my rear command post now and again in the Schwedt Castle. But as I was mostly not there, he contented himself with a report from one of my officers, drank his cognac and then went back to his own HQ.' In the end Skorzeny simply gave up taking any notice of the orders coming from his corps commander. There was too much to do on the sector of the front under his own command.

Somewhere around 7 February, 1945, he was forced to withdraw all of his outposts, except the one at the village of Nipperwiese, under heavy pressure. Day after day the Russians attacked the same three spots, obstinately ignoring their heavy losses, coming in time and time again in long grey-brown lines crying their 'hurrah' which was always the signal for an attack. And time and again Skorzeny's men threw them back. Indeed the motley division even managed to launch local counter-attacks against the Russians whom they now knew belonged to an elite guards corps.

But the Russians were getting ever closer. One day two of their T-34s even managed to get within 200 yards of the vital bridge across the River Oder which Skorzeny had not yet ordered blown in case it was needed for a German counter-attack. The tanks were finally stopped by Skorzeny's mobile flak units and the following infantry picked off one by one by Skorzeny's skilled snipers, well-sited in the ruins on the nearside bank of the river.

On another occasion two other Russian tanks managed to penetrate as far as his command post in the castle and started to fire round after round at its ancient stone walls. Hurriedly two of his battalion commanders collected the one-shot suicide weapon, the *Panzerfaust* bazooka, and rushed out to deal with the tanks themselves. While the rest of the scared headquarters staff watched breathlessly from the safety of their hiding places, the two young infantry majors stalked the tanks. Suddenly there was a breath-taking whoosh, a shower of red-hot sparks, and the hollow clank of metal against metal, as if a gigantic fist had struck the side of the nearest tank. It came to an abrupt halt. For a moment nothing happened, then smoke started to pour from it. Next moment the turret had been flung open and the crew were scurrying for safety in a hail of small arms fire.

Five minutes later the whole dangerous process was repeated and the second tank dealt with in the same way. The disaster had been prevented for yet another day.

So it went on, day after day, with the Russians getting ever nearer to the town. Desperately Skorzeny fought on. The last outpost on the other side of the river had to be evacuated. When the High Command heard of this, an irate radio message was sent demanding to know whether 'the CO of Nipperwiese [the outpost in question] has appeared before a court martial or been shot already?'

An enraged Skorzeny radioed back: 'The CO has been neither

sentenced nor shot'. And with that he went out with a group of his own SS paratroopers to rid himself of his bad mood by a little active service at the front.

But a shock was in store for him when he returned. The news was waiting for him that Himmler expected him at his head-quarters at Prenzlau and he was already four hours late for the appointment.

When he finally arrived at Himmler's HQ that night, the staff officers cold-shouldered him as if he had already been cashiered. Himmler's adjutant informed him coldly that the *Reichsführer* had 'had an attack of rage' because of his lack of punctuality and that now he 'must simply wait to be called'.

So Skorzeny kicked his heels drinking cognac brought by the orderlies, who at least were friendly. Finally he was called in to see Himmler, who was trembling and obviously angry and who immediately launched into an attack on his conduct. Accusations of insubordination and cheek, and threats of reduc-tion in rank and court martial came pouring out of Himmler's narrow mouth.

Skorzeny waited till his chief was finished, then he said calmly, 'The officer in question withdrew from the bridgehead [at Nipperwiese] on my orders.' Then suddenly his temper got the better of him and he told the *Reichsführer* what he thought of the High Command and its high-handed methods. 'Division Schwedt has received a devil of a lot of stupid orders from corps so far, but as yet not one kilogram of supplies,' he bellowed.

The sudden attack took the wind out of Himmler's sails. He calmed down, even inviting to dinner the man whom a little earlier he was going to court martial. Skorzeny had escaped with his rank – and probably his life – once more. By the time the meal was over Skorzeny had, in fact, managed to worm another assault gun battery out of Himmler and been promised all the help he needed. He never got it, but the promise had been made.

The battle continued in Schwedt, and his casualties started to mount as the Russians pressed closer. Grimly Skorzeny fought for every inch of the ground he had to give up; for him it was

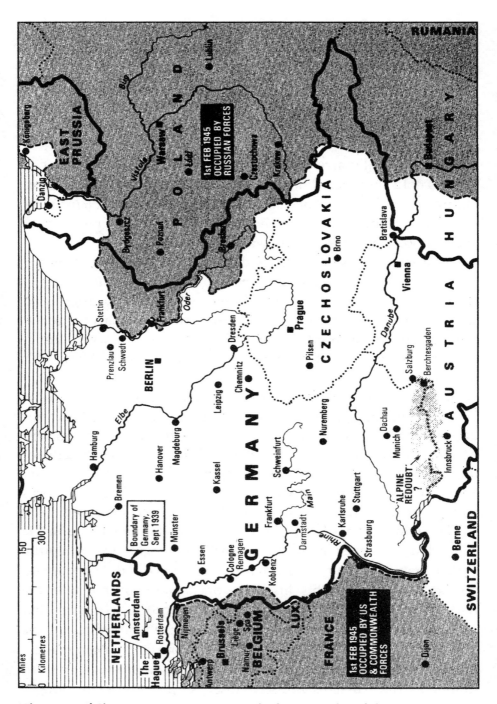

The area of Skorzeny's operations in the last months of the war

the holy soil of Germany, where the men he regarded as his forefathers had shed their blood to gain this territory for Germany from the Slavs over a thousand years before.

Once his mood of depression lifted when he heard of a BBC broadcast which had promoted him to a major-general long before the German Army Command had got round to rectifying that oversight. As the commander of a divisional strength formation, Otto Skorzeny reckoned he was entitled to the rank, but had forgotten to get round to filling out the requisite forms. The BBC had done it for him in its statement which said: 'The well-known SS chief Skorzeny who carried out Mussolini's rescue has been promoted major-general and charged with the defence of Berlin. He has thus become the most powerful man in the German capital . . . He has already started to liquidate all unreliable elements in the Berlin population.' It was a moment of lightness in an otherwise depressing February day for the newly promoted Major General Otto Skorzeny. Interestingly enough Skorzeny later found out that at the same time the BBC had broadcast its announcement, Hitler was indeed considering making him battle commandant of Berlin. He had almost magical faith in the SS colonel and thought him ideal for the job, but the staff turned it down. However, as Skorzeny wrote later: 'How did this news from the Reich Chancellery get to England so quickly?' He never found out the answer to that question.

But now his time as divisional commander of his 'European Division' was coming to an end. Just before he was relieved by Berlin, Field-Marshal Göring himself actually visited the Schwedt front. His belly somewhat shrunken and his medals conspicious by their absence, he proved a good jolly comrade who did not disdain talking and joking with the ordinary soldiers or paying a visit to the front, crawling up with the commando chief to the scene of the fighting.

Then one day, after his command post had been attacked by Russian fighters who launched a low-level sortie at his own office, shattering all of his windows but doing no damage except shocking his dog Lux out of its sleep, he received a message from

Berlin. It was the last day of February. The message read simply that he should be prepared to hand over his command within forty-eight hours and return to Friedenthal to await further orders. Hurriedly Skorzeny telephoned Berlin to ascertain what was to happen to the survivors of the men he had brought with him from Friedenthal. He was told coldly that they were to remain in Schwedt. He appealed to General Jodl, but the latter told him there was no use pleading. His men must remain and bolster up the defence of the bridgehead. Sadly Skorzeny took leave of his old veterans who had followed him loyally from the Gran Sasso to this last bridgehead. He would not see many of them again. The war was in its last phase. Germany would now have to pay back its debt in blood.

9

The Last Round-Up

At dusk on 7 March a usually very reserved Courtney Hodges, the distinguished-looking commander of US First Army, lost all inhibitions when he heard the news. One of his outfits, the 9th Armored Division's Combat Command B under the command of General Bill Hodge, had just seized a bridge across the Rhine. It was the famous Remagen railway bridge, an unexpected windfall. For the last few days his troops had been trying to capture bridges across the Rhine, but they had all been blown in his men's frustrated faces. Now a daring group of infantry under German-born Lieutenant Karl Timmermann had actually got a bridge!

At his headquarters in Spa, Hodges realized that this was a heaven-sent chance to crack the Western Front wide open. Throwing all his usual caution to the winds, he ordered his staff to push everything they had across the shaky structure. Then he telephoned his boss General Omar Bradley at his HQ at Namur in Belgium. 'Brad,' he said, trying to control himself, 'we've gotten a bridge.'

'A bridge! You mean you've got one intact on the Rhine?'

'Leonard [he meant the commanding general of the 9th Armored Division] nabbed the one at Remagen before they blew it up.'

'Hot dog, Courtney, this will bust him wide open! Are you getting the stuff across?'

'I'm going to give it everything I've got.'

'That's fine.'

Thus the last stage of the great six-year long conflict started. A short time later an enraged Hitler, who regarded the capture of the Remagen Bridge as almost a personal insult, summoned the only man he thought could still save the day: Otto Skorzeny. When he arrived there, Hitler was already in bed and instead he was received by General Jodl. Jodl gave him the task of destroying the bridge immediately with the aid of his specially trained frogmen, who were to transport explosive charges to the bridge which they would attach to its supports and blow it sky high. Skorzeny protested. He had had bad experiences with his frogmen a few months earlier when they had tried to destroy the Allied bridge at Nijmegen. Now he was expected to send his men of the 'Danube Frogman Group' into action in water whose temperature was almost at zero. Besides, the Americans had already extended their bridgehead several miles upstream and would naturally be on the look-out for saboteurs after their experiences at Nijmegen. He wrote later: 'This was the first time that I had not accepted a mission unconditionally.' He went away promising to do his best but not convinced of the viability of his mission.

As it turned out, he was right. The Danube group made the attempt several days later when the Americans had already established themselves firmly on the far bank of the River Rhine. Taking off one cold dark night, several of them simply disappeared as soon as they got into the fast-racing icy water. Others were picked up a little later in the sinister light of American searchlights perched on both sides of the river. Of the survivors who finally reached Remagen, not one escaped. They were all taken prisoner and, despite being able to attach their charges, their sacrifice was of no avail. The Americans had already built a pontoon bridge across the river. When in the end the Remagen railway bridge collapsed, probably owing to the initial damage when the German defenders had tried unsuccessfully to destroy it, the Americans continued to pump supplies across the Rhine by means of their pontoon bridge. All the effort was futile.

Soon afterwards Skorzeny was again summoned to the Führer's headquarters. The man who had once promised Germany that he would give the country a '1,000 Year Empire' now realized that his 'empire' was coming to an end after a mere twelve years. But now Adolf Hitler had completely abandoned reality, living isolated from the shattered world outside. Wearily he greeted his favourite commander with the words: 'Skorzeny, I have not yet thanked you for your stand on the Oder. Day after day it was the one bright spot in my reports. I have awarded you the Oak Leaves to the Knight's Cross. And I mean to hand them to you myself. Then you can give me a full account. For the future I have other work for you.'

With that the man who had dominated Europe for the last six years shuffled away, a broken dying man. Skorzeny was not to see him again.

Some time later he received an order from the Führer's HQ to go to Southern Germany and Austria, to report on the general situation and thereafter recruit the *Alpenkorps*, a force of desperate, diehard Nazis who would defend the mythical 'Alpine Redoubt', the area of mountains between Austria and Bavaria where worried Allied Intelligence officers and gullible Germans believed there was to be a last ditch stand by Germany's most fanatical soldiers.

Skorzeny's family was still in Vienna as well as two of his special Friedenthal commando units so that when he heard during the course of a lunch with Field-Marshal Schorner, who was in charge of the southern sector of the German front in the East, that the Russians had already entered Vienna, he decided immediately he would begin his 'tour' in the Austrian capital.

After six hours of hard driving he started to approach the suburbs of his native city. Everywhere German soldiers were streaming westwards in disorderly retreat, their spirit broken and their main concern only to save their own skins. As Skorzeny's driver honked his way through the unruly crowd, Skorzeny's rage began to mount, until he could not contain himself when he saw a group of able-bodied soldiers riding on a horse-drawn cart while behind them trailed the pathetic figures of the wounded. Angrily he ordered his driver to stop and, springing out, tried to halt the cart. When the sergeant in charge did not obey his command to stop, he reached up, grabbed him by the collar and slapped him hard across the face. The sergeant stopped.

Skorzeny pointed to the furniture heaped up at the back of the cart, which the soldiers had obviously looted, and bellowed, 'Now throw out all that furniture and make room for the wounded!' Then he indicated the girl who was balanced on the back of the cart, and added, 'And if she wants to go along with you, she can walk.'

Then, to make sure that the sergeant obeyed his orders, he snatched the man's pistol away and gave it to the nearest wounded man. 'See that he only loads up the wounded,' he commanded.

The incident with the NCO convinced Skorzeny that the situation in the East was desperate. As he wrote later: 'In such a critical situation and scared for their bit of life, people drop their masks and become supreme egoists.' But he had no time to consider the implications of this critical situation; he had to get to the capital. He jumped back into his vehicle and ordered his driver to push on.

It was dark by the time he reached Vienna. To his relief he discovered that his two special units had already left westwards. Now he felt he could devote himself to his family. His mother's house was already badly damaged and she had left two days earlier. The same applied to his brother. Now as he got closer to the centre of the city, the roar of battle grew steadily louder. Near the beautiful Schönbrunn Palace, he stopped two elderly policemen and asked them what the situation was.

They sprang to attention and reported with a grin, 'Herr Obersturmbannführer, we are the defence line of Vienna.'

Skorzeny paid a brief visit to his old factory which was still working and then drove on through Russian-held streets to the fortress headquarters of General von Bunau, who was in charge of the defence of the capital. Swiftly he put the general in the picture, telling him he had seen a lot of Russians during his journey across the city but no German soldiers. 'When I get out,' he told the General, 'I shall tell the Führer that Vienna is lost.'

Bunau then asked him if he would like to see Baldur von Schirach, at one time head of the Hitler Youth and now 'defence commissar' of Vienna. Skorzeny replied in the affirmative, and he was soon ushered into Schirach's much too elegant 'command post', lit by candles. The man who had imbued Germany's youth with its fanaticism and single-minded loyalty to the Nazi cause smiled when he entered. 'You see Skorzeny,' he said, 'I've only candle-light to work with.'

Skorzeny nodded and then repeated the statement he had made to Bunau. 'I haven't seen a single German soldier. The road blocks are unmanned. The Russians can walk in whenever they like.'

'Impossible!' Schirach said in disbelief.

Skorzeny told him that he should drive around and have a look at the situation himself. But the ex-Youth Leader would not believe him. Using a plan that had been the basis for Prince Starhemberg's relief of Vienna from the Turks in 1683, Baldur von Schirach explained that he had two divisions at his disposal. 'One division is coming from the west and another will cross the Danube to reinforce us. We'll hold the Russians.'

Skorzeny looked at him in disbelief. He knew there were no troops available. The ex-Youth Leader was operating with ghost formations which did not exist; indeed the whole atmosphere in the cellar had, as he wrote later, 'something ghostlike about it'.

But he said nothing and took his leave of Baldur von Schirach, whose last words to him were, 'Here I shall fight and die.' In fact the man who had sent so many German youths, blinded by the illusions he had given them, to their deaths, surrendered tamely and survived to spend the next decade-and-a-half in prison.

Soon thereafter Skorzeny dictated a radio message to Hitler which read:

'On the streets leading from Vienna to the West I found more or less chaotic scenes and I propose to take forceful action there.

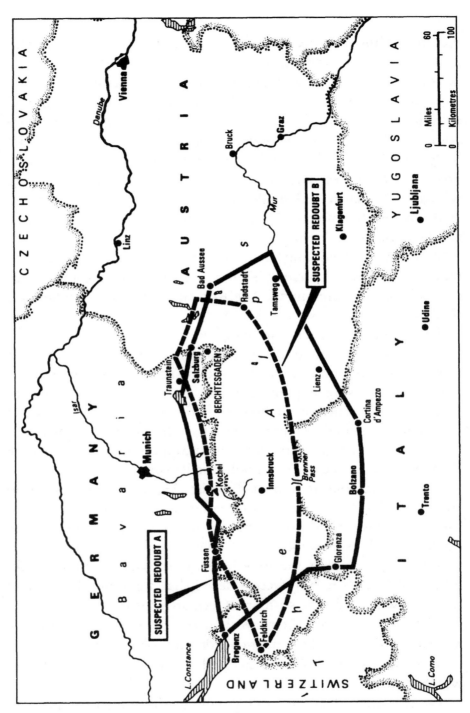

Presumed area of the Alpine Redoubt
where Skorzeny had intended to make his last stand

94

Vienna practically defenceless and will fall into Russian hands this morning.'

At dawn on that morning 11 April, 1945, he drove over the Viennese Floridsdorf Bridge for the last time, stopping briefly for a final look at the burning city of his birth, now beginning to be obscured by the growing Russian artillery barrage. Something broke within him. As he wrote after the war: 'I suddenly lost my old drive.'

The war had another five weeks to go, but Skorzeny was no longer interested. Dutifully he rallied those of his special commando units whom he could still find and directed them to march upon the Alpine Redoubt. In the meantime, before he went to the redoubt himself, he set about clearing the roads in Upper Austria of the refugee columns so that they could be used by the troops. At the same time he ensured that checkpoints were set up everywhere in the region where soldiers who had been cut off from their units could report and be formed into new fighting formations.

A few days later Radl appeared suddenly at his headquarters with some 250 men from Friedenthal. Skorzeny was overjoyed to see his old friend and they decided it was time to retreat into the Alpine Redoubt. At local army headquarters, they were told to collect as many of their units as they could and take them into the mountains. Here they would wait for the regular troops to retreat into the redoubt, where they would be formed into the 'Alpine Corps', with Skorzeny's men providing the nucleus of this 'last ditch' fighting force.

Together Radl and Skorzeny drove into the area to find out exactly how much had been prepared for the defence of the Alpine region between Austria and Germany. They were in for a bitter disappointment.

They searched everywhere for some sign of organized defence, without success. All they found was a few horse-drawn carts filled with provisions, a couple of half-completed positions and rusting machinery intended for the underground munition factories which had never been built. The Alpine Redoubt did not exist save in the imagination of Gauleiter Hofer, who had first dreamed up the idea, and in the nightmares of Allied Intelligence officers, who feared they might be fighting German partisans in the difficult terrain years after the real war had ended. Sadly Skorzeny realised that he had come to the end of the road. They had neither the men nor the equipment to fight a protracted battle in the Alps. For him the war was over. The question now was, what was he going to do? A friendly air force pilot offered to fly him out of the beaten country to neutral Spain, but Skorzeny declined. He had no time for commanders who left their men in the lurch when the going got tough.

In the end he released his men, taking particular care that his volunteers from Allied countries such as Belgium and France had a decent chance of escaping, and fled into the mountains with Radl and a few of his old comrades. Taking up residence in a hut on the Dachstein mountain he lazed away the days after 8 May, 1945, until he learned from his peasant contacts in the valley below that the Americans were searching for him. Already they had arrested scores of suspects who they mistakenly believed were Skorzeny himself or were connected with him.

Skorzeny decided that he had better surrender and sent a letter to the nearest American commander advising him of his presence on the mountain. There was no answer. He sent another. Again no reply. Meanwhile Radio Luxemburg, the Allied-controlled broadcasting station, appealed to its listeners to help find the 'most wanted man in Europe'. The newspapers took up the hue and cry. And still the Americans down below in the valley seemed uninterested in their prominent 'guest'. Another letter was sent. Again no answer.

Finally Skorzeny was successful. One day he went down into the valley with Radl, his first general staff officer Captain Hunke and interpreter Lieutenant Peter.

He had made an arrangement with the Americans for a jeep to be waiting at a particular bridge. It was eleven days after the capitulation when he and his three men walked into the American HQ in Salzburg, fully armed and still in German uniform, to give themselves up. But surrendering was not that easy. The sergeant to whom they surrendered had never heard of Skorzeny. But if they felt they were important, he told them, he would provide them with a jeep and they could surrender to divisional headquarters.

So they set off for the Divisional HQ, with an American driver who told them, after Skorzeny had given him his name, 'If you're Skorzeny, you'd better take a drink. Tonight they'll hang you.' In Salzburg the man deposited them outside an Allied controlled hotel. Still no one seemed interested in them. Finally a major appeared and told them to go elsewhere to pick up orders. And all the time they were still armed.

But finally someone realized whom the division had captured. Skorzeny was asked to enter a villa for an interview with two young American officers. Bewildered and yet amused, he did as he was requested. Hardly had he taken a seat than windows were flung open on all sides and machine guns were thrust in to cover him.

Now the Americans were no longer casual. He was disarmed and stripped, and a rapid examination was carried out to ascertain whether he had poison hidden about his person. Then he was bundled into a jeep, with an MP holding a machine pistol to his face. Covered by armoured cars the jeep was driven to Salzburg where, with his hands tied behind his back, he gave his interview to the representatives of the Allied press. The Skorzeny legend was beginning to grow. 'Skorzeny certainly looks the part,' wrote the female correspondent of the *New York Times*. 'He is striking in a tough way: a huge powerful figure. The "Beast of Belsen" is something out of a nursery in comparison.' And for the sake of her female readers she added as an afterthought, 'He has blue eyes.'

A British reporter present wrote: 'It was thought best to keep Skorzeny with his hands manacled behind his back. When he was given a cigarette, it was lit and he had to have the ash shaken off. A glass of water was held to his lips.'

But in spite of their gushing prose, the reporters were seeking an answer to a very serious question, one that was going to haunt Skorzeny for many months to come: 'Why did you try to murder General Eisenhower?' They were referring of course to the exploits of his jeep teams during the Ardennes offensive and the statements made by some of the captured commandos.

Skorzeny told them, 'If I had ever been ordered to attack Allied GHQ, I should have made a plan to do so. If I had made a plan I would have carried it out. And no one would have been left in doubt about what I was trying to do.' But they simply did not believe him.

As the *New York Times* reported in its next day's issue: 'Handsome, despite the scars that stretched from ear to ear, Skorzeny disclaimed credit for leading the mission to murder members of the Supreme Command.' It was obvious that the journalist, in common with most of his fellow correspondents present, already knew that Skorzeny was guilty: he had really tried to kill Eisenhower and failed.

10

Escape or Die

After two years in a prisoner-of-war camp Otto Skorzeny was brought to trial at Dachau in front of a war crimes court. The charges against him were numerous; they ranged from the alleged slaughter of some one hundred captured Americans, through the use of American uniform during combat by the men under his command to the 'plan' to assassinate General Eisenhower. In late July, 1947, he was brought before Colonel Rosenfeld of the US Army who during the Battle of the Bulge had worked in Field Security and who now was functioning as judge or legal officer in most of the 'atrocity' trials to be held in the late 1940s in Number One Courtroom in the former German concentration camp.

The allegations against Skorzeny were put by Colonel Rosenfeld, a sharp-faced, bespectacled officer who, reading from a document, detailed the charges. But the Austrian only heard point number one – that his unit had killed and mistreated American prisoners of war. Figures could not be given exactly but more than one hundred were supposed to have suffered. Where had this alleged massacre taken place and when?

Skorzeny was never to find out, for the charge was eventually dropped. Presumably the American prosecution felt that Skorzeny was involved in the alleged massacre at Malmédy because one or two of Skorzeny's jeep teams were present at the Battle of the Bulge. The other charges, however, were still held against him, though by now Skorzeny had obtained the services of a very able lawyer, Lieutenant-Colonel Robert Durst.

For four days after he accepted the brief to defend the German 'war criminal' an unsmiling Colonel Durst cross-questioned his client to ascertain his degree of guilt or his innocence. Later Skorzeny admitted it was the toughest grilling he had ever undergone. But after four days, Durst walked into his cell, shook him by the hand for the first time, and smiled: 'I am sure of your innocence on every charge. Now I know that you have nothing to hide I shall fight for you as if you were my brother.' His new attitude shocked Skorzeny, who until now had felt that Durst was on the side of the prosecution and had been allotted to him just as part of the democratic farce. But Durst kept his word. He fought tooth and nail for his German client, even though the German lawyers who volunteered to defend Skorzeny without a fee told the latter that he should not trust the American officer completely. Skorzeny ignored their advice. He put his trust fully in the American, and it was rewarded. Even when Skorzeny's trusted adjutant appeared on the witness stand and testified for the prosecution that the 150th Brigade had recruited English-speaking personnel for special tasks during the Ardennes battle, Durst kept up a spirited defence of his client.

And even when one of Skorzeny's men, an ex-supply captain, turned into what Skorzeny regarded as a traitor and gave evidence for the prosecution that Skorzeny had distributed poisoned bullets to his men during the Ardennes battle, Durst did not lose heart. Nor did Skorzeny. The bullets in question, he knew, were modelled upon ones taken from two Russian prisoners who had tried to murder a German general in Russia. He had ordered them distributed to any of his men who felt that they could not stand captivity; with them they would be able to escape their captors by a quick suicide, as the bullets fired into any part of the body would bring rapid death. In fact Skorzeny himself had one in his possession during the last months of the war. But how could he prove that the bullets were intended for use not against the enemy but against oneself?

In the end he smuggled a note out of the camp to Radl who

was located in the ordinary prisoner-of-war camp outside the top security Dachau compound. He wanted a sample of a bullet to show the court. Radl did not let him down. The next morning he found the bullet in question in the centre of his morning hunk of black bread. In court that morning Durst held up the bullet for the supply captain's inspection: 'Is that your poisoned ammunition?' he demanded.

The startled court craned forward, as did the captain, to have a look at the surprising piece of evidence. It was an ordinary bullet with a red ring around its base.

The captain nodded hesitantly. Yes, that was the kind of ammunition that Skorzeny had distributed to his men before the Battle of the Bulge. Then Colonel Durst forced the supply captain to admit that in reality it was simply a waterproofed form of normal ammunition and that the poisoned pellets were entirely different. The charge was dismissed and the trial went on. In late August Skorzeny took the stand himself to explain his actions in the Battle of the Bulge and, in particular, to defend himself against the charge of allowing his men to use American uniforms during the offensive.

For two days he explained his plans and their execution during the battle; he did not deny that he and his men had been prepared to wear and had actually worn American uniforms during the course of his operations. His defence of his actions was that he had not been alone in doing this; before him virtually every other Allied nation had used the same dodge. In the case of the Americans they had worn German uniforms on several occasions, for instance during the attack on Aachen; and it was this occasion which had given Hitler the idea of having Skorzeny's men wear American uniform.

During the course of this two-day marathon in the witness box, Colonel Durst raised the question of the alleged plot to murder General Eisenhower. Immediately the President of the Court ruled Colonel Durst out of order and the question struck from the rolls. Thus the Eisenhower plot was never satisfactorily explained and that particular 'canard' was to stay with Skorzeny for ever (being brought up time and time again in the years to follow).

At the end of the two days Colonel Durst and Otto Skorzeny had conjured up the picture of a new type of warfare which in the ever-changing technological 20th century was always ahead of the laws intended for the more sedate 19th century. In other words the Hague Conventions for land warfare drawn up in the first decade of our century and based on the experiences of the previous one had simply no relevance to our own time with its atomic weapons, area and strategic bombing, and, naturally, its various types of irregular warfare. To solidify his case, Colonel Durst called a surprise witness, Wing-Commander Forrest Yeo-Thomas.

Skorzeny had already read about the legendary Yeo-Thomas, the 'White Rabbit' as he had been called in French Resistance circles, in Kogon's *SS Start*, but thought that he had been killed in the war. Now the short sturdy figure in RAF blue appeared to be very much alive, in spite of his long years in the Resistance and the hard slog in Whitehall trying to convince Churchill and others of the need to support the new French underground movement. In the end he had been captured, taken to Buchenwald from where he had escaped, leaving a corpse in his place, and walked to the Allied lines. Immediately after the war he had given evidence at the Buchenwald war crimes trial which had resulted in twenty-two of his guards being sentenced to death.

Skorzeny must have wondered whether this was the right man to give evidence for him. There seemed to be no reason why he should show any favour to his former enemies who had treated him so badly during his period of captivity.

But Skorzeny, like the rest of the court, was in for a surprise. Without hesitation, and fully aware of the meaning of his testimony for Skorzeny, he told the court, 'My comrade was in prison at Rennes in Brittany. I reconnoitred the jail and bribed one of the guards to find out when rounds were made and the general procedure ... Then I put some of my men who spoke German into German uniform and secured copies of German papers required to take a prisoner out of jail. We stole a German car and I also had a van rigged up to resemble a prison van. The plan was to ring for the gatekeeper and show him false papers. We would drive in with the German car and then bring the van in and stall it so that they could not close the gate.'

Durst let him explain the raid in full detail, waiting for the moment when he could make his own point.

'The men in German uniform, one of them disguised as an officer, were to go into the guardroom. If the prisoner were not delivered to us on sight of the papers, if there were any hesitation, we would dispose of the guards quickly and silently.'

He paused and Colonel Durst asked, 'Did you obtain German uniforms for this purpose?'

'Yes'.

'How were they obtained?'

'The details I could not tell you. I gave instructions to obtain uniforms by hook or by crook.'

Durst then led him up to stating, after being asked whether he and his men were armed when they wore German uniforms, what they did.

'To prevent danger of discovery, what would the practice be?' Durst asked.

Wing-Commander Yeo-Thomas now glanced around the court before replying. He said softly, 'Bump off the other guy.'

Colonel Rosenfeld's case had vanished. As Yeo-Thomas came down from the witness stand, Skorzeny and the other defendants in the case got up from the cage and stood silently and stiffly to attention; it was the only token of respect and thanks they were in a position to offer to the former enemy who had saved them, though later Skorzeny sent him a note of thanks, to which Yeo-Thomas, now director of Molyneux, the Paris dressmaker, replied, 'You did a damned good war job. I'm sure you will get off. In any case I have a flat in Paris if you should need somewhere to lie up.'

A few hours after Yeo-Thomas's evidence, the case against Skorzeny was dismissed, but in spite of being acquitted, he was still not released. He was transferred to a 'de-nazification' camp at Darmstadt. Every time his case came up for review it was postponed for some reason or other. The months passed. When his case was postponed for the seventh time Skorzeny had had enough. Writing to Yeo-Thomas, he asked him for his advice. The reply was laconic and to the point: 'Escape,' he wrote back.

The testimony of Yeo-Thomas did it! The court could not find a man guilty of dressing his men in enemy uniform in action when a senior British officer had done the same in France with his Resistance fighters.

On 11 September, 1946, the *Stars & Stripes*, the US Army's newspaper in Germany, carried the banner headline, 'Skorzeny Cleared on All Counts'. The prosecution fumed, but the Panel could do nothing; the 'Most Wanted Man in Europe' had been cleared by the US Army Tribunal. Still the prosecution found pretexts for keeping Skorzeny behind bars, though, in theory, he should have been released there and then. It was stated that several other Allied countries had made application to have Skorzeny extradited for alleged war crimes. Russia, Czechoslovakia and Belgium, among others, wanted him and, in due course, even the Germans of the Zonal governments did too, so that he could go through the compulsory de-Nazification process.

These demands didn't worry him particularly, save the one from Russia. There he knew he'd receive no trial. In Moscow he would be interrogated, squeezed of all the information he possessed about his undercover operations in that country and then quietly shot by a firing squad of green-capped NKVD officers (forerunners of the KGB). But somehow – Skorzeny didn't know how and by whom – the Russian application was rejected. Already, unknown to the prisoner, someone very powerful in the Allied camp was watching over him, in case his particular talents were needed in the future.

So, while he languished at Dachau, Frankfurt and finally at Darmstadt, when he he had been transferred to German custody, he made a cheeky application to join the US Army's Historical Branch's team currently writing up the history of the Second World War. The basis of many statements from both Allied and enemy participants would later form part of a series of official tomes on the great conflict. (The last of these histories dealing with the US Seventh Army appeared as recently as 1994, fifty years after the events described in the book and at a time when most of the participants were long dead!)

So finally, after nearly a decade of living on his nerves, Otto Skorzeny, still a kind of prisoner although he had been acquitted of the criminal charges brought against him, lived a relatively easy life in comparison with the majority of fellow Germans outside the camps who were, up to mid-1947, on the verge of starvation. He received the same rations as his, at first, American guards and as the months passed and he made no attempt to escape he was given leave to visit a mistress and, in due course, his wife and daughter. And all the while he was kept fully up-to-date on what was going on on the outside through his network of informers and ex-comrades of the *Waffen SS*. There was only one fly in the ointment, or so it seemed to him, the application for his extradition by Prague. As 1946 gave way to 1947, it was clear that that unfortunate country was coming more and more under the influence of the communists. If the Czechs succeeded in the application, Otto Skorzeny didn't need a crystal ball to know what his fate was to be. The Czechs would hand him over to their new Russian masters very quickly. As 1947 gave way to 1948 and the Cold War began in earnest, Skorzeny started to think seriously of escape.

And there were those among his erstwhile enemies who would be only too glad if he did so. For by now the clandestine war in the shadows between East and West was already raging and these unknown new friends knew that in due course they would be able to use a man like Skorzeny with his knowledge and contacts on both sides of what had already become known as the Iron Curtain. All the same, these would-be helpers knew they had to be careful. To most Americans the ex-SS Colonel, friend of Jochen Peiper, now sitting in his Dachau prison, wearing the red jacket* of those condemned to death for his part in the infamous 'Malmédy Massacre', the man who had tried to assassinate Eisenhower, was the Nazi war criminal *par excellence*. They decided to let Skorzeny get on with his escape under his own steam and with as little help from them as possible. They'd approach Skorzeny when the time was ripe, and it wasn't ripe just yet.

The Czechs, urged on by the Russians, pressed their case. Skorzeny was informed by his old SS comrades, who had the information from the Americans, that the latter would delay the paperwork on the extradition request for a few more weeks. In the meantime Skorzeny had better get out of the German-run internment camp at Darmstadt.

In Hanover the former SS officers worked all out to prepare for Skorzeny's escape. In the meantime he was volunteering for more and more outside working parties, cleaning up the bomb-damage in the city that housed the editorial officers and printing plant of the *Stars and Stripes*.

Skorzeny had long maintained that it would give him the greatest of pleasure to confront the German De-nazification Tribunal. There he would lay his cards on the table and tell the Tribunal all he knew, including, perhaps, details of those German turncoats who were now prominent figures in the pro-Allied administration of the American Zone of Occupation. But now Skorzeny realized that he couldn't wait for the Tribunal to convene. Still, he was not going to slink away from the Darmstadt Camp like a thief in the night. Boldly, he faced the Camp Commandant and told him that he was going to escape at the first available opportunity. The Commandant's reaction is not recorded, but, whether the Commandant was going to take counter-measures or not didn't worry Skorzeny. Time was running out for him and he *had* to go.

---

* It was an old German tradition to dress a condemned man in the infamous red jacket, so that he would be immediately recognizable.

On 27 July, 1948, three ex-SS officers in civilian clothes, driving a car supplied by Skorzeny's American friends, set off on the long journey down Germany's bombed roads and through her ruined cities from Hanover to Darmstadt. At Würzburg, not far from the internment camp, they stopped for food, to change into olive-drab uniforms and replace their civilian plates with the tags of the American Occupation Forces. Then they continued their journey, now dressed as 'white mice', as the Germans called the military police contemptuously, on account of the American cops' white helmets and gaiters.

Some time later three bogus military policemen entered the Darmstadt internment camp's guard house and stated briskly, 'We are here to take the prisoner Skorzeny to Nuremberg for his hearing scheduled for tomorrow,'

The civilian guard, intimidated by the 'American captain', glanced briefly at their forged documents and then, without further ado, brought Skorzeny out. Flanked by two 'white mice', with the captain in the lead, the little party walked out of the camp gate and disappeared – for ever. It would be the last time that Skorzeny, who was to be a wanted man for the rest of his life, would ever again see the inside of a prison.

The agents of the mysterious German 'Gehlen Organization', of which we will hear more later, and their new masters, the CIA, under the command of a future director of that service, Allen Dulles (the brother of the all-powerful US Secretary of State for Foreign Affairs, John Foster Dulles) had done their work well. They had secured the escape of a very important new employee-to-be.

But as yet Otto Skorzeny didn't know that. After three years behind bars when others had determined his life, he was in charge of his own fate once more. But what could an ex-commando, notorious as he was, and a member of a beaten and discredited nation to boot, do in a post-war Europe? No one in his right mind, especially if he belonged to one of the victorious allied powers, would want to employ an unrepentant Nazi, still wanted on charges of war crimes by the Czechs. And after what he had been through in the war, mixing with Nazi and other Fascist *prominenz*, he certainly could not go back to his tame pre-war profession of engineer in Vienna, currently under four-power controls. The Russians would whip him off to some gulag or other within forty-eight hours of his reaching his native Austria.

For a while he hid out in Germany, using the alias of Rolf Steinbauer in Düsseldorf, working for the mysterious Gehlen Organization (and naturally the newly formed CIA, though he didn't know that *then*) from a rundown plumbing shop.

Then his hiding place was discovered and reported to the German authorities, who wanted to arrest him. Naturally 'Steinbauer' was informed of their intentions well in advance. Skorzeny decided to 'take himself out of the dust', as the German expression has it. He fled across the border into Austria. Surrounded by former SS officers, who guarded him night and day, he instigated divorce proceedings against his first wife. That done, he disappeared again, feeling it was time that he left Europe for a while. Otto Skorzeny's amazing postwar career had begun.

II

Post-War Operations

For some two years after his flight from Allied internment little was known of Skorzeny's whereabouts. Some maintained that he had fled to the high mountains of his native Austria where he had hidden back in May, 1945. There the Russians carried out a search for him. He had been spotted in Italy, but he had been in transit, heading for no one knew exactly where. The Jewish Hagannah organization, very active in Italy in those days, also looked for him; the Jewish agents knew that he had contacts among radical Arabs who wanted to throw the Jews back into the sea. But their efforts there, and in Egypt, drew a blank. Skorzeny seemed to have vanished into thin air. Even Spain, where Franco had already openly welcomed Nazi fugitives from Allied justice, revealed no trace of him.

But one dictator, thousands of miles away at the other side of the Atlantic, *had* made the fugitive welcome. He was Colonel Peron, the Argentinian strongman. Not only did the two men share the same political views, but Peron also had a great deal of interest in German money which had been smuggled out of Nazi Germany, when defeat began to seem inevitable for the Third Reich. (Not only Switzerland, as has been recently revealed, but the South American republic were to be storage places for huge sums of gold and money, most of it turned into real estate by investing in local firms.) Peron was not the only one interested in that money – 'Himmler's' or 'Bormann's' gold as it has been termed at various times – Otto Skorzeny was too!

One major figure who had access to the money was no less a

person than the President's wife, Evita. Known as the 'woman with the whip' because she supposedly whipped political prisoners, Evita had learned early on of the existence of these huge sums – eight hundred million dollars in bank deposits, 2,500 kilograms of gold, 4,600 carats of diamonds and other precious stones. All this would go a long way, Skorzeny reasoned, to founding a new Reich and presumably to line his own pockets.

But by the time Skorzeny arrived in Buenos Aires Juan and Evita Peron were acting as if the assets were part of their own personal fortune. Those Germans sent to watch over the cash were rapidly losing control, so Skorzeny speedily made plans to rectify the situation.

Naturally he was received with honour by Peron as the man who had rescued Mussolini. But while he basked in the adulation of Peron, Skorzeny shrewdly assessed the situation in Buenos Aires and it didn't take him long to realize that Eva was the real brains behind the government – a tough-minded woman, who was both ambitious in the manner of a slum child (which she was) and exceedingly greedy.

As he recorded, 'One report I received at that time was that the only way she could be softened up was to get her into bed when she was lonely.* After being in prison for several months and not able to get near a woman, I replied that *I* was the ideal man to soften her up.'

Having grasped the situation at the top, Skorzeny began to make a covert play for the woman who held the key to the Nazi gold. But he was careful enough not to display any obviously open interest in her undoubted sexual charms. He helped her with her police reforms. He took the Peronista secret police in hand (perhaps he taught them some old Gestapo tricks; afterwards they were regarded as the most brutal in the whole of

---

* At this time Evita *was* lonely. Peron, whose sexual appetite was waning, had begun to take up with nubile teenagers who wouldn't criticize his performance as mature women such as Evita would.

South America). Certainly he made sure that they were on constant lookout for any attempt on the lives of the Perons. Once indeed Skorzeny personally foiled an attempt on Evita's life. He apprehended at pistol point two suspicious characters who, according to him, were planning to murder her. Knowing Skorzeny's past record, it is conceivable that the whole would-be murder plot was staged to impress 'Little Eva'. At all events, afterwards she always regarded him as her hero, the man who had saved her life.

According to one German witness at the time, Herr Bracker, who was Peron's German financial adviser and who, naturally, knew about the missing Nazi gold, they became lovers. The expatriate German maintained that 'They were very close. I know for certain that they often went on two-or-three-day trips together, supposedly to inspect various government installations. Actually, they were holed up in one of Evita's secret residences, either near the ocean or high in the mountains. She was fascinated by his reputation, his huge size and his manliness. He was always interested in beautiful women, and if they had power and influence, so much the better. In Evita's case his interest was much greater because she controlled the Bormann treasure.' (Martin Bormann, Hitler's 'Brown Eminence', was the Nazi official who had supposedly arranged for the German gold to be sent to South America in the first place.)

Some commentators maintain that in the first years of the fifties, before Evita's death, Skorzeny managed to get *one hundred million dollars* from her of the Nazi gold, which he shipped back to Europe to finance his various Fascist projects and used to help to found a Fourth (Nazi) Reich. But as with all major money transactions (as we have seen recently with the revelations about Nazi gold being sent to Switzerland and Spain), it is always very difficult to trace the transfer of such large sums of money.

But by now, with Skorzeny already developing his clandestine connections in Europe, as we shall see, the time had come for him to leave South America and whatever German treasure still remained there. Evita had developed cancer and was wasting away, so much so that Peron refused to visit 'that bag of bones'.

So unperceptive was he that Peron didn't realize that his power over the people depended upon Eva. After all she was the 'people's champion' and maintained for Peron the support of his rank-and-file working class adherents. Skorzeny, however, realized that the death of Eva would sound the death knell for the Peron régime, which indeed it did. Three years later in September, 1955, Skorzeny, from Madrid, would arrange the escape of Peron in a Paraguayan gunboat from South America to the Spanish capital, where he could keep a careful eye on the ex-dictator until he had outlived his usefulness.

Unfortunately he could not do the same for his supposed one-time mistress. Eva was embalmed after her death and in due course was smuggled out of Argentina to start a 20-year odyssey, being shifted in her coffin from place to place in order to avoid capture by her enemies. In recent years it has been reliably reported that during this period the body suffered many base indignities including sexual abuse by some of her young guardians who wanted to boast later that they had had intercourse with 'Evita', forgetting to mention in their *macho* pride that the sexual liaison had taken place *long after she was dead*!

But in 1952 Skorzeny had other things on his mind than Eva Peron. For by that time he was working for that great nation whose President had once exploded angrily that he was 'the most dangerous man in Europe'. And now, indirectly, he was in the employ of the CIA – strange bedfellows indeed.

In the spring of 1945, a tall, cold-faced German general with the red stripe of the Greater German General Staff running the length of his trousers decided the war was lost and the time had come to make his separate peace. He was a man who had spent most of the war in remote headquarters hidden in Russian forests, surrounded by a strange mixture of middle-aged highly intelligent German staff officers, bold young lieutenants who mostly hailed from the German-speaking families of the Russian Baltic and rough-and-ready soldiers in nondescript uniforms, devoid of badges of rank, most of whom could only speak broken German.

He was General Reinhard Gehlen, head of the strangely named 'Foreign Armies East', a man who liked to live in the shadows and was rarely photographed. He was the commander of Hitler's Intelligence services on the Eastern Front, whose daily assessments of Russian strengths were usually the basis for Hitler's next move.

On 4 April, 1945, Gehlen met his senior officers, all dressed in civilian clothes, in a small inn in Saxony and made a startling suggestion. They would ship all their top secret papers on the Russians, the products of many years of war, to the Bavarian Alps. He had already found a remote mountain fastness for his team there. There they would sit out the rest of the war and avoid being split up among various POW camps after they had been captured. Once Gehlen had assessed the immediate post-war situation, he would offer themselves and the vital information in their possession to their erstwhile enemies, the *Amis*, as they called the Americans. We don't know the immediate reaction of Gehlen's officers to this amazing plan to start working for an enemy against whom they had been fighting only a few days before. What we do know is that in the end they accepted it lock, stock and barrel.

Thus it happened that the 'Gehlen Organization' started working for American Intelligence, the OSS, the forerunner of the CIA, almost immediately after the collapse of Hitler's Reich. Soon it was clear that the General of Intelligence had made a correct decision. Within a few months the Americans were actively engaged in the war in the shadows against their one-time ally. The Cold War had begun.

Over the next few years the Gehlen Organization, with its contacts, German and foreign, reaching to Moscow itself, became the prime source of American Intelligence on all things Russian. Even when the Gehlen Organization became the official Intelligence gathering institution of the new Federal Republic of West Germany now named the B.N.D. (*Bundesnachrichten-*

dienst), it still remained primarily in the pay of 'Foggy Bottom', the home of the CIA.

Naturally one of Gehlen's senior advisers in matters of long-range penetration and sabotage was Skorzeny. After all, the two so different officers, one bold and flamboyant, the other cold and calculating, had worked together during the war, with Skorzeny running anti-Russian para-teams as far east into the Russian Soviet Empire as the Ural Mountains, supposed by the communists to be absolutely safe.

Skorzeny helped with the infiltration of British agents into Eastern Baltic ports in torpedo boats manned by sailors of Hitler's former navy. He assisted again with similar agents parachuted into Albania on behalf of the British MI6 – and again, as was the case with the Baltic op, the agents were betrayed to the KGB by the arch-traitor in the pay of Moscow, Kim Philby.

Naturally all the operations in which Skorzeny was the guiding spirit were not failures. Gehlen and Skorzeny could afford to use the 'blunderbuss method' in their ops. There were agents enough. Adventurers, renegades, patriots, criminals – they queued up to take part in these very risky undertakings, where it was certain death to be captured, either at the hands of the Russian executioners or by means of the 'L-Pill', the lethal cyanide pill which they usually kept concealed among the teeth at the back of their mouth. (Later it became standard Russian interrogation technique to run a needle and thread through any suspect's upper lip so that he couldn't bite down hard and crush the hidden 'L-Pill'.

Unfortunately, however, Skorzeny, like so many Austrians of his time and age, was an anti-semite. After all Hitler,* Eichmann and the last head of the SS security services, Kaltenbrunner, were all virulently anti-Jewish, and by now, in addition to his work for Gehlen, Skorzeny had been hired to work for the new rulers of Egypt.

---

* It is often forgotten that Hitler was an Austrian citizen for most of his life, only becoming a German in 1928 in early mdidle age.

In 1952 Colonel Gamal Abdul Nasser, an admirer of Hitler who had worked for German Intelligence against the British in the Second World War, had taken over power in Egypt after the fall of King Farouk, the enormously fat ruler of that country who was more interested in pornography (he had one of the largest collections of dirty pictures and sex objects in the world) than the welfare of his poor peasants.

Because of Skorzeny's anti-Jewish attitude and the great deal of money being offered him he accepted Nasser's offer to work for him in Cairo with alacrity.

The CIA, which was indirectly funding Skorzeny in his Cold War activities, apparently had no objection to the appointment – at first. After all Nasser was seen by the American agents as the Middle East's prime bulwark against the Russians. Under Nasser's leadership the other Moslem Middle Eastern countries would fall into line and stop any further 'Red' advances in that strategically vital area. Indeed, in 1952 the CIA under Allen Dulles had agreed with Nasser that the revolution against King Farouk would take place in easy controlled stages, with the gentlemen from Foggy Bottom naturally doing the controlling.

Gehlen was brought in to help out in Egypt at the start. He recruited a team of 200 ex-SS and Wehrmacht officers under the command of *General der Artillerie* Wilhelm Farnbacher. Later the middle-aged General, who had commanded the isolated fortress-seaport of Lorient for months after the Germans had been thrown out of Occupied France and had actually continued the war against the Franco-American besiegers for *four days* after the official peace had been signed on 8 May, 1945, remarked disdainfully that he would 'never have accepted the appointment if I had known the kind of men I was going to command'.* Soon the 'defender of Lorient', who was awarded the Knight's Cross of the Iron Cross by Hitler personally, was going to be even more disgusted by his 'bedfellows' when Skorzeny turned up at his HQ. For Skorzeny and some of Farn-

---

* In conversation with the author.

hacher's SS officers had been recruited for unorthodox military duties. It was to be their task to organize Nasser's secret service, and police, to direct espionage and sabotage and to carry out surveillance of the new Egyptian strongman's many enemies within the country, such as the feared Moslem Brotherhood; and these hard-boiled ex-SS officers under Skorzeny's command, many of whom had just been released from Allied imprisonment, were not very fussy about the methods they employed. Their methods were straight out of the Gestapo training manuals. As General Gehlen himself put it, 'We found Arab countries particularly willing to embrace Germans with an ostensibly "Nazi" past.' It was not surprising. Hitler had persecuted the Jews and anyone who had helped to do so was particularly welcome in an anti-Israeli Cairo, where the dead Führer was revered. As Dr Noureddine Tarraf, Minister of Health and one of the most important supporters of the Egyptian nationalist cause, put it at the time, 'Hitler is the man of my life. The German dictator had been an ideal leader who dedicated his life to the realization of his noble ambition. He never lived for himself but for Germany and the German people. I have always wished to live like him.'

Skorzeny felt at ease among the younger Egyptian officers, some of whom had worked actively against the British during the war under the command of Major Nasser and Lieutenant Sadat, later Egypt's President. Employing men such as SS General Dirle-Wanger, known as the 'Butcher of Warsaw', SS Major Hermann Lauterbach, onetime commander of the Hitler Youth, and the infamous SS Colonel Eichmann, Skorzeny speedily went to work against Nasser's internal enemies, but most importantly against the Jews. He set about training the first Palestinian terrorists who have remained a thorn in the Israelis' side to this very day. Defying a secret weapons ban on Egypt, which was to prevent her taking part in any Arab coalition war against Israel, he smuggled the latest automatic weapons from Belgium, Italy and the like into Egypt. With them came the technicians of death, men who had pioneered the deadly gases which the Nazis had used in the concentration camps and those nerve gases, which *fortunately* Hitler didn't employ against the Allies, but against which the West had had no masks or protective clothing. Other scientists were the same men who had worked under Werner von Braun in Peenemunde and had helped to develop those missiles which had devastated London and Antwerp in the last year of the war. And naturally there were those who promised Nasser the most horrific weapon of all, the nuclear bomb.

Slowly becoming aware of what was going on in their new protégé's country, the CIA still believed they could foster Nasser's ambitions in the Middle East and at the same time protect Israel, now supported by the powerful Zionist lobby inside the USA. The cynics might wisecrack that 'a Zionist is a Jew who pays another Jew to send a third Jew to Israel'. All the same these same maligned Zionists had a great influence on American foreign policy.

Knowing that Skorzeny was behind much of the Egyptian effort, the CIA pundits believed that his hatred of Russia would make him work to keep the communists out of the Middle East. They believed further they could nip any Egyptian aggression against the new Jewish state in the bud.

But as so often in the nearly fifty years of its existence, the American Intelligence Organization was proved wrong. The withdrawal of Anglo-American funds to Egypt to help build the vital Aswan Dam, which Nasser thought would be a lasting memorial to his greatness, infuriated him. The West's strong condemnation of Skorzeny-trained Egyptian and Palestinian terrorists' activities on Israeli territory didn't help either. In a sudden volte-face, which caught the Americans completely by surprise, Nasser turned to the Russians for help.

Interestingly enough, Skorzeny, the red-hater, played a rôle in this about-face. In a dispatch from the Cairo-based US embassy, it was revealed that an associate of Skorzeny's, Dr Wilhelm Voss, had long been playing the rôle of Egyptian go-between on Cairo's behalf.

It states: 'Dr Voss has been playing a double game since

October, 1952. Among the group of German military experts closely co-operating with each other are Dr Voss, Skorzeny, Major Mertins and Colonel Ferchl. The latter was a member of the German General Staff.' Surprisingly enough, Ferchl was the only member of those elite German officers of the General Staff released by the Russians from prisoner-of-war cages after 1945. Did this mean that one of Skorzeny's senior colleagues had been a Russian agent all along, foisted on him in Egypt for the purpose of watching what these unrepentant Nazis were doing there?

As the US Embassy commented in its report: 'Ferchl and Mertins are in touch with two Russian women . . . Voss has four Czechs working for him. He pretends these are Sudeten Germans and has asked the German embassy to give them passports – *refused.*'

It was clear that all was not well in Cairo and that the German experts, imparted with the knowledge of the CIA, were playing both ends of the field. But Skorzeny weathered the storm for a while. Indeed he made a small fortune from the money transactions between Nasser and his new masters, the Russians and the Czechs, working for the former. Yet still the Americans continued to support him and his German experts. They had no other option. US Assistant Secretary of State Averell Harriman, who during the war had been Roosevelt's adviser in London, maintained that the Germans should stay in Egypt. As he said, 'The departure of German scientists from Egypt could lead to their replacement by teams of Soviet scientists able to accomplish the same tasks and would not alter in any way the situation in the Mideast, other than increase Egypt's dependence on the USSR.'

The crunch in Egypt, as far as Skorzeny and his influence was concerned, came in 1965 when Nasser invited Walter Ulbricht, head of the German Democratic Union, to Egypt. The West German government protested. Nasser refused to withdraw his invitation. Bonn reacted angrily. It broke off diplomatic relations with Cairo, established full diplomatic contacts with Israel and stopped all economic aid to Egypt. That dealt the death blow to the efforts of the Germans in that country and Skorzeny's rôle there had come to an end.

Indeed the final events in Egypt marked the end of Skorzeny's international operations. He had crossed the Americans, lost the faith of right-wing Germans, especially those in the govenment in Bonn, incurred the undying hatred of the Israelis (at the back of Skorzeny's mind there was always the possibility that he might be abducted to Israel by the *Mossad*, just as his onetime associate and fellow Austrian, Adolf Eichmann, had been) and was now confined to Madrid, where the ageing dictator Franco would probably be succeeded by a liberal King, the future Juan Carlos, already being groomed for the rôle by the *Caudillo* personally. What would happen to him when Juan Carlos took over? He wasn't a Spanish citizen. All he possessed was a Nansen passport given to those who were stateless. Would Juan Carlos, perhaps embarrassed by this fascist relic in Madrid and dependent on the support of the Americans, have him quietly deported as an undesirable alien? Where would he go? What would he live from? It must have seemed like the end of the road. All he had to sell now was the story of his life. But he had sold that, or as much of it as he wanted to tell, nearly a quarter of a century before.

When the present writer approached him on the subject, his return correspondence was full of references to the monies he might make for 'my co-operation in an account of this nature'. The man who had once made the headlines with the stories of his daring and boldness was now writing what amounted to begging letters. Two years before his death, he was writing to an acquaintance: 'It is a pity that I have no time at the moment to write a new book, but I have in mind to write one day a book about all the political and military persons I have met. You would be astonished to know all the names of kings, presidents of states, dictators and field marshals I have known.'

Surprisingly enough, in the light of the desperate situation in which he now found himself, plagued at the same time by pains in his back that for days he could not even walk, Skorzeny still kept secret a story that would have put everything else he had ever written into the shade. The story, even though it might well have been proved not altogether truthful in the end, would have created a world sensation. It would have kept him in luxury to his dying day. *It would have been the story of how, nearly twenty years before, he had successfully blackmailed no less a person than Britain's great wartime Prime Minister, Sir Winston Churchill.*

12

The Churchill Ploy

Dawn, 26 April, 1945.

In Italy the war was almost over. The Western Allies were advancing on a broad front through the Po Valley, heading for the Austrian border, where the link-up with the US 7th Army advancing through Bavaria into Austria would take place. Then the war in what Churchill had termed 'the soft underbelly of Europe' (the troops called it bitterly, 'tough old gut') would finally be finished after nearly two years of bloody fighting.

Now the rats were leaving the sinking ship and in the North, contrary to the wishes of the Anglo-Americans, who wanted stability and no communist interference as there had been in Greece with British troops battling Greek partisans, the Red brigades were waiting to take over.

The day before, the exhausted and fatalistic Italian dictator, whom Skorzeny had rescued in what now seemed another age, had telephoned his long-suffering wife, Donna Rachele, and told her that he was 'at the last stage of my life, the last page of my book'. He had begged her to take their two children to Switzerland where they could 'build a new life'.

The previous evening they had met for the last time. In the growing darkness he had handed her some papers, including papers from Churchill. He hoped these would get her over the frontier. He told her, 'If they try and stop you or harm you, ask to be handed over to the English.' At the moment Mussolini couldn't have realized this was the worst advice to give to anyone who knew about the 'Churchill papers'.

Now in a heavy drizzle the little Italian convoy, guarded by picked SS men, mostly from Skorzeny's *Jagdkommando*, scurried hither and thither, while Mussolini desperately attempted to save his neck and that of his young mistress, dark-haired Clara Petacci, who had insisted she should accompany her lover even if it meant death at the hands of the partisans. With them the Mussolini entourage took another closely guarded suitcase, filled with vital secret papers. It was a case that Skorzeny, now far off in Vienna, knew something about, for he had seen it before. It had accompanied the Duce when the former had flown the Italian dictator to safety in 1943. Now that case was being watched closely by one of Skorzeny's picked men, *Obersturm-führer* Franz Spoegler. This handsome young German had befriended Clara Petacci. She liked him a lot and trusted him. But Spoegler had other things on his mind than a romance with Clara, whose lover was no longer able to perform too well: his own safety and those vital Churchill letters, which Skorzeny guessed might well open some very important doors in the dangerous months to come.

Some time after he left on this desperate mission to save his neck, Mussolini's little group of Italians and SS officers were joined by a large German convoy of twenty-eight trucks, filled in part with German infantry supposedly heading home to the Reich. This increased force came under fire from Italian left-wing partisans who were everywhere and brought to a halt on the narrow country road. The Italian force was led by 22-year-old Count Pier Luigi Bellini delle Stelle, who wasn't a communist but whose father, a Cavalry colonel, captured by the Germans in 1944, had died of maltreatment in a German prison. Hence his presence at the head of communist partisans.

The German commander, *Hauptmann* Otto Kisnatt, who spoke Italian, tried to negotiate with the Italians blocking the road, maintaining that he had permission from Milan, the partisan HQ, to proceed on his way. Bellini didn't believe him. After several hours of impasse, firing broke out and some of the Italian and German members of Mussolini's party were wounded. It was about then that the former Duce was recognized, disarmed, saying to his captors, 'I won't do anything.' Obviously he was resigned to his fate.

The partisans assured their captive that nothing would happen to him and Mussolini was left under guard together with a brownish-yellow leather case. He asked one of the guards, named Lazzaro, to look after the case. In a low voice he added significantly, 'Those are secret documents. I warn you. They are of the greatest historical importance.'

Lazzaro looked through them swiftly. To him they didn't seem particularly important, save for a lengthy correspondence with Hitler. He couldn't read German so he didn't know how important those letters were.

For a while Mussolini was left alone with Clara Petacci. Bellini assured her she need not have any fears. He would look after her and she could spend the night with her lover. In her gratitude she tried to kiss the young Count's hand, crying, '*Grazie, grazie*'. He pulled it back, red with embarrassment.

At eleven o'clock Bellini started to get worried. He had received no further orders as to what to do with his prisoners. So off his own bat he decided to move them to a safer place in the small town of Dongo. It was here that Mussolini and his mistress met their final end and it was here, too, that the mystery started which has puzzled historians ever since: WHO SHOT MUSSOLINI AND CLARA, AND WHY?

The traditional account is this: In Milan a large group of mostly left-wing partisans made a decision. They would send an armed band under the command of a Colonel Valerio (his *nom de guerre*) to bring Mussolini to Milan. When the decision had been made and the non-communist partisan leaders had left, the communists remained, to be told that Palmiro Togliatti, head of the Italian Communist Party, had made an overwhelming decision. Mussolini and his mistress would be shot without trial. The assassin would be Colonel Valerio.

To forestall the Allies and any attempt on their part to take Mussolini alive, the Communists signalled Allied HQ at Siena:

'THE COMMITTEE OF NATIONAL LIBERATION REGRET NOT
ABLE TO HAND OVER MUSSOLINI WHO, HAVING BEEN TRIED
BY POPULAR TRIBUNAL, HAS BEEN SHOT IN THE SAME PLACE
WHERE FIFTEEN PARTISANS WERE SHOT BY FASCISTS.STOP.'

At dawn on 28 April, 1945, the fifteen heavily army partisans
under Valerio, who had fought in the Spanish Civil War and was
a dedicated Communist, set off. At 1.30 that day Bellini, still in
charge of Mussolini, was informed that a car filled with armed
partisans had arrived in the town square of Dongo and
demanded the surrender of the place.

Bellini arranged an interview, after having been told that
Dongo was surrounded by armed Communist partisans and that
he and his men were heavily outnumbered. The meeting didn't
go well. The 22-year-old Count knew that he was at a disadvan-
tage with his handful of guards and he felt that Valerio was up
to no good. Soon he found out that he had been right.

Valerio demanded a list of the Mussolini party under Bellini's
command. Reluctantly Bellini gave him it. Taking his time
and full of his own importance, the self-styled Communist
Colonel went down the list with a stub of pencil, while Bellini
sweated it out. Valerio paused half-way down the list and
said with an air of finality, 'Benito Mussolini – *death*!' He
made a cross against the name and continued, 'Clara Petacci –
death!'

The young officer looked at him aghast and cried, 'She was
only his mistress.'

Valerio flushed angrily. 'I know what I'm doing,' he shouted.
'I'm the one to decide.' Then he added that he was in a hurry.
He had to get back to Milan with the bodies before dark.

It was four o'clock when Valerio and the other partisans burst
into the house in which Mussolini and his mistress were held. 'I
have come to rescue you,' he yelled.

'Really,' was Mussolini's sole reply.

On the bed Clara started pawing through her pile of clothes.
Impatiently wanting to get away, Valerio asked her what she

was looking for. She replied, tears in her eyes, 'My knickers.' She was partially naked beneath her skirt and blouse. Significantly, she had sent Skorzeny's man, *Obersturmführer* Franz Spoegler back to her original home to fetch more clothes for her. With him had gone that supposedly vital valise with its key papers.

Valerio said the knickers didn't matter. Nor did they. Soon the young woman would be subjected to terrible sexual abuse, which the mob would have carried out whether she was wearing knickers or not.

They were hurried outside to a waiting partisan car. With two heavily armed guards on the running board and two curious fishermen running after it, the old car ground its way up the steep hill toward Azzano. The car had gone only a matter of a few hundred metres when the driver stopped at the iron gate of a large shuttered villa.

Valerio dropped over the side. Crouched low, as if sensing danger, he crept cautiously to the nearest corner, peered around it and then called back that the rest of the party should hide in some trees next to the gate. Valerio came back and for what seemed an eternity, though it could have been only a matter of moments, a strange silence descended on the little group.

Suddenly Valerio shouted at the top of his voice, 'By the order of the general headquarters of the Volunteers for Freedom Corps I am required to render justice to the Italian people!'

Clara knew what that meant. She flung herself, arms extended, in front of Mussolini protectively. 'No,' she screamed, 'he mustn't die!'

'Move away if you don't want to die too,' Valerio yelled.

Clara moved to the right. The Duce said nothing. Valerio aimed at Mussolini's chest and pressed the trigger of his machine pistol. *Nothing!* There had been a stoppage. He grabbed his pistol and tried again. Once more *nothing!* It seemed as if some God on high didn't want Mussolini to die just yet. He called to one of his comrades, 'Give me your pistol.'

This time the ex-dictator's luck ran out. At a distance of some three metres so that he could hardly miss, Valerio fired a full magazine from the Mas 7.65 pistol at Mussolini. Mussolini crumpled on to his knees and then pitched forward onto the damp earth. He was dead before he hit it. Valerio swung the smoking pistol round on Clara, who had followed her lover into exile and now into death.

Early next morning their bodies were found near a garage, not quite completed, in the centre of Milan. The mob soon learned who they were, as they lay in the gutter like bundles of rags. Screaming with rage and overcome by a strange kind of atavistic blood lust, they went to work on the hated dictator and his mistress. The men urinated on Mussolini as the Italian sign of infinite contempt and then began beating the body with sticks, pushing and jostling each other in order to launch vicious kicks at his dead face.

The ultimate indignity was inflicted on Clara. Old crones squatted and urinated in her open mouth. Twenty-three years before, Mussolini had marched on Rome, armed with little more than an idea, and seized power. Now his 'New Romans', as he had called them proudly, had not only murdered him, they were pissing on him too.

Back on 29 July, 1943, in an operation that remained a German secret until the end of the war, the Research Institute of the German Post Office managed to tap the underground cable crossing the Atlantic which linked Britain to America and succeeded in unscrambling the scrambled phone connection habitually used when Roosevelt in Washington spoke to Churchill in London about secret affairs of State. It was a great technical achievement. Now the German operatives, glued to their earphones, listening to the conversation, distorted a little by the crackle of static, heard something of great significance. It was all connected with Italy, which was secretly discussing an armistice with the Western Allies who had landed in Sicily earlier that month.

'We don't want proposals for an armistice to be made before

we have been definitely approached,' said Churchill. 'That's right,' Roosevelt agreed.*

Then they talked about the fate of the missing Mussolini. Both agreed he would end up 'on the hangman's rope'. But how? Churchill was in favour of a show trial, which would be a 'healthy lesson for the Nazis'. Roosevelt was against the trial. Such a legal process might affect the coming presidential election when he would run for a third term. 'Couldn't he [Mussolini] just die suddenly?' Roosevelt urged suddenly. He made the point that several of Churchill's enemies had died 'abruptly' in aeroplane accidents.

Roosevelt went on to say, 'I think that if Mussolini died while he was still in Italian hands we would be best served . . . If we agree to get rid of him while he is still in their hands . . . there'd be no doubt who had killed him . . . That wouldn't upset my Italian voters here in the States.'

Churchill wasn't convinced. He said, 'I can't believe that the votes of a handful of Italians in your country can influence your decisions.'

Roosevelt didn't pull his punches. 'If I'm not nominated,' he replied, 'then I won't be elected . . . If I lose, our alliance might break up. Stalin will make a separate peace with Germany. Then Hitler will turn his full anger on Britain and, without help, what can you do?'

In itself that overheard conversation is of only fleeting interest. What is of lasting interest is Roosevelt's belief (and naturally that of other powerful people) that Churchill wouldn't hesitate to use even murder to get rid of people who stood in the way of his policies. The mysterious murder of Admiral Darlan in North Africa in 1942 was cited by Churchill's enemies and critics as one example of the way his political opponents were dealt with. The still unexplained crash of General Sikorski of Poland just off Gibraltar in a plane is another.† Was Mussolini's quick dis-

---

* These excepts are the author's translations of the original German translation of the Churchill-Roosevelt conversation.
† Darlan stood in the way of the Allies unifying the French in North Africa who had sworn allegiance to the pro-German Vichy government. Darlan

patch, before he could start relating the secrets he knew, another? Were the partisans under the command of 'Colonel Valerio' indirectly under Churchill's control? Or was that traditional account of how the Italian dictator died the true one?

Churchill was by nature an old-style *Realpolitiker*, who often felt that end justified the means. His domestic policies often showed that, in particular his pre-war custom of changing parties when their policies – and his rôle in them – didn't suit him. But Churchill was a great Englishman and, in many ways, a noble and moral one. It seems to the present author that it would be *impossible* for such a man to stoop to murder. Besides, what would be the point? What conceivable hold could Mussolini have on him? Yet there are many, and not just young academic revisionist historians out to make a name for themselves by re-writing the history of the Second World War, who feel that Churchill *would* stoop to murder to protect himself. For years now, in particular in Italy, there have been persistent claims that the traditional account of the murder of Benito Mussolini is fake. He wasn't killed by Italians at all, but by the perfidious English *on Winston Churchill's orders*. And if we are to believe Skorzeny, he had in his possession those long-missing documents which would prove just that!

---

himself had been a senior member of that government. Sikorsky, the Pole, was violently anti-Russian and would not go along with Churchill's plan to sacrifice part of Poland as the price of keeping Russia in the war.

13

Blackmail!

Two days after Mussolini and Clara Petacci were done to death two twin-engined RAF light bombers appeared in the sky above the Albergo Bazzoni in the town of Tremezzo, where the two had last been spotted. The locals watched them with interest and without fear. Why should they be afraid? The *tedeschi* had gone and the whole area was in the hands of the partisans. The war in the 'tough old gut' was about finished. The two Mitchells circled the little hill town several times, as if searching for something. Some of the locals knew that Mussolini and his mistress had spent some time in the Albergo Bazzoni before they had set off on that fatal car journey. Could that be the reason for the Royal Air Force's presence? But before they could answer that puzzling question, things started to happen – *fast!*

The two RAF planes came zooming in at the lowest height possible for accurate bombing, as if they had a specific target. A myriad deadly black eggs began falling from their blue-painted bellies. In panic, the local civilians dropped to the ground, hands pressed to their ears.

The bombs hurtled towards their target. They started to explode on all sides with a throaty crump. In an instant the peaceful little town was transformed. Mushrooms of black smoke ascended slowly to the sky. The RAF had done a good job. The Albergo Bazzoni had been well and truly bombed, leaving dozens of dead and wounded behind. But why? Was there something at the inn which the British authorities wanted destroyed before it was discovered by the advancing American troops? Why else should this harmless, undefended mountain township be attacked at this final stage of the war? Again a question without an apparent answer.

But for those who support the theory that Churchill was behind the murder of the former Duce the bombing of the Albergo Bazzoni fits into the general picture of the plot all too well.

As Professor Renzo de Felice, one of Italy's most renowned historians an biographer of Benito Mussolini, has maintained quite recently (1995), the Valerio assassination team, sent by Milan to deal with the ex-Duce, arrived at Dongo too late for Mussolini had already been assassinated. To cover up their failure, they had pumped further bullets into the corpses of Mussolini and his mistress and then had them transported to Milan where they were put on display to prove that the communist partisans had been the ones who had dealt with the tyrant. In his book Professor de Felice, who holds the chair of modern political history at the University of Rome, provides no evidence to support his claim. *La Guerra Civile, 1943–45* simply makes the mind-blowing statement as a matter of fact. Another popular historian, Franco Bandini, goes a little further. He maintains that the two had been killed *prior* to the arrival of the communist partisans by British agents to prevent Mussolini from revealing the secret negotiations the former had held with Churchill. The bombing of the Albergo Bazzoni, two days later, was to ensure that any other documents pertaining to these talks left behind there after the executions would be destroyed. In essence, according to the Italian historians, no evidence had to survive which would link Churchill with the former Duce.

So what really happened?

According to Bruno Lonati, aged 76 an ex-partisan, Mussolini and Clara were shot by an assassination team under the command of an Englishman, Captain Malcolm Smith. The Englishman, who is now dead, was born in Sicily, the son of a British businessman, and some time before the war, because he knew the country and spoke fluent Italian, 'John' (as he was known to

Lonati) was recruited as a member of the British Secret Intelligence. This has been confirmed by British historians of the period. Smith was a member of MI6.

Later, Lonati's controversial account of what really happened seemed to be confirmed by the discovery of the memoirs of another partisan, Franco Magni, who disappeared mysteriously two years after the assassination. According to Magni's memoirs, *Rebels of the Resistance in Pre-Alpine Lombardy*, this is what happened: 'They [Smith and three other gunmen under his command] entered the room where Mussolini and Clara were held. They led them out at around 10 p.m. A short time later shots were heard.' As Lonati records it: 'The Englishman told me that we would have to shoot them and that it would have to be one of us Italians to fire. We went out of the house and after following the path for 200 metres, I fired several sub-machine gun shots without warning, aiming at the heart of Il Duce. Almost simultaneously 'John' opened fire on the woman. It was just after 11 am on 28 April, 1945.'

But then it appeared a second 'execution' took place, carried out by the partisans from Milan under 'Colonel Valerio', whose real name was Walter Audisio. It is not known whether Audisio-Valerio was present in Milan when the only proven contact between the British and the communist partisans took place. At that time Massimo Salvadori, an agent with the SOE – he was the British liaison officer to the partisans – told the partisan council that when Mussolini was captured, and he would undoubtedly be captured soon, he should be killed to avoid the 'unwelcome' publicity of a trial. But now to Valerio's chagrin Mussolini was already dead. Was Valerio concerned that he had failed to carry out the advice given by a leading British representative? Or was it that Valerio knew that it would be a tremendous propaganda coup for the illegal communist party, attempting to take over the industrial north of Italy, if Mussolini appeared to have been assassinated by a member of that party, namely himself?

At all events a second 'execution' seems to have been carried out by Valerio and in due course he was to be officially credited by the standard communist party history of that period as the one who had pulled the trigger.

Over the last half-century the events of those last days of April, 1945, have engendered claim and counter-claim, affirmation and denial, which have blurred the issue considerably. But one thing is clear as far as the British involvement is concerned. Salvadori, the SOE agent, *did* advise the communist partisans to get rid of Mussolini by assassination. He was backed up by the statement taken long after the war from another SOE agent, Captain Richard Cooper. When Cooper returned from the war he brought with him as a *souvenir de bataille* a black dome-topped hat, complete with tassel and fascist emblem, of the type worn by high-ranking *fascisti*, including the Duce. When asked by his son, a retired SAS officer, whether it was taken from Mussolini in that last week of April, Captain Cooper wouldn't talk about it, though, as his son recorded, 'He was always happy to talk about other things'.*

Even at a much lower level the British seemed to be aware *before* the assassination that something drastic was going to happen in the Milan area. Military Police and Field Security Police were alerted to stand by for trouble. It wasn't specified what exactly this trouble was, but Military Police units were sent post-haste to Milan at that time from as far away as Ancona on the Italian coast some 200 miles from the city.†

It is clear then, despite the distortions of time, and those of sensationmongers, that the British were involved in the assassination of Mussolini and that the British agents who took part

---

* According to Mr Cooper Junior the hat has now disappeared, given to the landlord of a pub 'somewhere in Devon'. *Sic transit gloria . . .*
† Following up a lead in this context in 1996, one elderly man who had taken part refused to reveal any details. A month later when the present author again tried to interview him at the remote East Riding seaside town where he lived, he was told that the former lance-corporal in the Military Police had suddenly upped and left for the Isle of Man. *He hadn't left a forwarding address!*

acted on orders right from the top. Now we have seen from that tapped telephone conversation between Churchill and Roosevelt of 1943 that, at that time at least, Churchill favoured a 'show trial'. It was Roosevelt who suggested that Mussolini should be got out of the way by unorthodox means. How, he didn't specify.

Yet nearly two years later Churchill seems to have been behind the plot to deal with the captured Duce by assassination, speedily and without trial. What could have changed his mind so drastically (if it was indeed changed)? The answer is the existence of the 'Churchill Papers'. But by 1 May, 1945, when the Allies had overrun the area where Mussolini and Clara Petacci had been murdered, those 'Papers' – and they clearly existed, though we know little of what they contained and whether they really covered the period from 1940–1944, as some revisionists suggest – had vanished. Where had they gone?

In 1939 *Diplom-Ingenieur* Otto Skorzeny volunteered from Vienna to join the most elite regiment of the *Wehrmacht -die Leibstandarte, Adolf Hitler*. It was the regiment filled with superfit blond giants (one tooth filling meant that any volunteer would be turned down), clad in black, who had been recruited by Sepp Dietrich, Hitler's bodyguard and old Party bullyboy, to guard the Führer at his various residences. These were the men of Nazi Germany's first Guards regiment (though privately they called themselves somewhat cynically 'the asphalt soldiers' due to the fact that they always seemed to be goose-stepping down Berlin's broad streets on some ceremonial parade or other).

At first the overage and overweight Viennese with no military training was accepted into the 'Bodyguard' only as a probationary. But in the end he was commissioned as an engineer-transport officer and took part in the campaigns in Holland and Russia where he fell sick and was invalided out of the formation.

But the *Leibstandarte* had always been something special for him and he had enjoyed a friendship with many of the Regiment's then junior officers. During the long bitter conflict that followed his departure from the *Leibstandarte* it was reconstituted three times over due to casualties. Many of those junior officers had long vanished into the greedy maws of the God of Battle. But there were many of the veterans, 'the old hares', as they called themselves, who *had* survived. Now these men, who had become colonels and generals and divisional commanders by the end of the war, sat behind 'Swedish curtains', as they called the prison bars in their soldiers' slang, as convicted war criminals and members of a 'criminal organization' (the SS). There was Colonel Peiper, to whom Skorzeny had tried desperately to break through in the Battle of the Bulge. He was in Landsberg, ironically the same prison where the Führer had written *Mein Kampf* back in the twenties. Dietrich, now a colonel-general and former Sixth SS Army commander, was also facing life imprisonment, as was another old comrade, General 'Panzer' Meyer of the Hitler Youth Division, who had fought the British to a standstill at Caen. He had been sentenced to death for having killed Canadian POWs. But his sentence had been commuted to life imprisonment. Now the unrepentant Nazi languished in Verl Prison in Northern Germany.

The fact that these *'Nur-Soldaten'*, as they called themselves, i.e. soldiers pure and simple, languished in prison because of the crimes of the Party officials, angered Skorzeny. The Americans, due to the pressure put on them by the Korean War and the need to have a stabilized Germany in Central Europe to stop the march of Russian communism westwards, had already begun to release some of these war criminals. But, as Skorzeny saw it in the early fifties, Britain was the stumbling block in the process of having them all released, at least his key friends. It was time for him to put the pressure on the British and, not to put too fine a point on it, resort to blackmail if necessary.

1952 was election year in the UK. The Labour Government of 1945 had about run out of ideas – and money. Even to non-partisan oservers it was obvious that the time was ripe for a change in government. Churchill, although he was an old, tired man in his mid-seventies, decided to run for office once again. As he confided to cronies, it was more for the benefit of the

Conservative Party than anything else; he thought his candidature would secure a new five-year term for the Tories.

But as the pre-election campaign began, ugly rumours about Churchill's wartime activities started to circulate in London. In essence they maintained that the PM had had dealings with the enemy, in the shape of Mussolini, right up to April, 1945. This meant that while British soldiers were dying in their thousands in North Africa and later in Italy, their political master was corresponding with that Italian who had taken his country into the war on the side of Nazi Germany. It was the sort of scandal that would destroy not only Churchill's great wartime record, but which would kill any chance of the Tories forming the new government. Could it be possible that Churchill, who had strictly forbidden any secret dealings with the Germans in the form of the anti-Nazi resistance, right throughout the war, had been dealing with Mussolini all along? Left-wing newspapers such as the now defunct *Daily Herald* sensed a great political scandal in the making. Reporters scurried back and forth over Western Europe checking out stories like that of a former Lt-Colonel de Toma who had seen the Churchill corespondence in Italy (the Donna Rachele letters, which Mussolini had assured his wife would ensure her safety back in April, 1945). He maintained that he remembered one letter from the British Premier to the Duce offering French-controlled Tunisia to Italy. France, which was on the verge of defeat that May, would be given the Belgian Congo (Belgium had already been beaten by the Germans) as compensation.

As de Toma, and others trying to get on the bandwagon at that time, recalled, the correspondence had started using Dino Grandi, the ex-Italian Ambassador to the Court of St James and later head of the Fascist Grand Council, as intermediary in April, 1940. He was the one who had transmitted the letters back and forth until he had been instrumental in deposing the Duce in 1943. Among the correspondence, which had started off with Churchill's desperate attempt to keep Italy out of the war that April, there were others to such people as Umberto, the Crown

Prince of Italy and later, for a little while, King of that country. According to these informants, including one in Spain, who offered to deliver another batch of 'Churchill Letters' to the British Ambassador in Madrid for one hundred thousand dollars (a fortune in those days), Mussolini had penned his final missive to the British Prime Minister on 21 April, 1945, exactly one week before he was murdered!*

It was in the midst of all these rumours that the Grand Old Man surprisingly decided to go to Venice. Skorzeny, who knew of the Spoegler's valise and another one that Mussolini had clutched to his chest during that dramatic flight in 1943 out of his mountaintop prison, stated that he had waited to deal with Churchill, who had refused to help his old comrades 'until an opportune moment and that moment came when the old man wanted to be re-elected to office.'

In August, according to Skorzeny, the two men met in Venice. Skorzeny's only companion and eyewitness was a certain Paul Foerster. He was explicit about what transpired at that strange meeting between the great statesman and the piratical adventurer. He stated afterwards, 'Sir Winston received some wartime items he wanted very badly and in return we received hope that some of our comrades in prison might obtain an early release.'

A year later Churchill was elected and quite definitely things started to move fast for the imprisoned SS men. Franz Alfred Six, who had been slated to run an occupied Britain in 1940 and a one-time superior of Eichman, was released. Edmund Veesenmayer, another old comrade of Skorzeny's, followed. To cries of protest and great outrage in Canada, 'Panzer Meyer' followed, going straight from Verl prison to a meeting of old SS comrades, declaring arrogantly, 'We do not intend standing at the back door [of the prison], nor at the rear entrance which is for messengers and servants. We intend to enter the state through

---

* Churchill later wrote in his account of the Second World War that he had only once corresponded with Mussolini in that period when he had sent a telegraph to the Duce urging him not to enter the war on Germany's side.

the front door. Yes, my comrades, the Federal Republic is our state.' Typical 'Panzer Meyer' and typical of the new aggressive mood among the former members of Hitler's Black Guards.

Skorzeny had, indeed, presented the '*Alte Kameraden*' with a rallying point by his bold piece of blackmail. But it was a flash in the pan and was soon forgotten, as was the affair of the 'Churchill Papers' (though it was to be another two years before the furore died down).

Skorzeny returned to his nefarious dealings in the Middle East, while Churchill, being informed by the British Ambassador in Madrid that yet another 'Italian'* in Spain had offered to sell the British the 'Churchill Papers' for one hundred and fifty thousand pounds, snorted in exasperation, 'In the words of the Duke of Wellington – *publish and be damned!*'

---

* One wonders if these various 'Italians', domiciled in Spain, were in fact employees of Skorzeny.

14

End Run

When in 1973 Skorzeny wrote that it was 'a pity that I have no time to write a new book', he did not realize that he had muffed the chance back in the early fifties to write a book that would have had a much more shattering effect than any of his post-war coups. But by 1973 it was too late and as always Skorzeny was more interested in his own affairs than those of other people; he couldn't visualize a book in which he only played a minor role, limited to that of a blackmailer. It was a personality defect. He had always demanded centre stage.

Anyway there were much more compelling reasons for his not writing that book. He was getting too old and forgetful. More seriously, he was being plagued by his back even after the two tumours had been removed. Some days he had to stay in bed absolutely still and drugged to the eyeballs with painkillers.

Naturally his old comrades and new admirers of the various Neo-Nazi organizations which had now sprung up all over Europe (and in the United States) still believed he was active in the cause of fascism. He was supposed to be involved in large-scale gun-running in Africa, aiding those Nazis who had escaped to the Middle East and South America after the war via the so-called Odessa organization (in fact it was called, by those involved, *die Spinne*, the spider, which had its web every-where*), and helping presumably CIA agents in their attempts to kill Fidel Castro in Cuba.

* Even today there is a fortress-like 'holiday camp' on the Spanish coast,

In fact Skorzeny was too ill to do anything but mark time. When Peron was returned to power in Argentina in 1973, Skorzeny wasn't strong enough to join him. But he did make certain that Eva Peron's body, hidden for the intervening years, was returned to him. However, when Peron fell from power two years later, the body again disappeared to begin that strange odyssey which this time fortunately did not take it out of the country. It was one of Skorzeny's last acts to ensure the safety of his one-time lover's corpse. Today she lies at peace in Recoleta Cemetery.

But now time was running out for the ailing man. He weakened visibly. He was shaken by fevers. His big body shed flesh at an alarming rate. Those dark eyes grew faint and the whites turned a light yellow, an indication that the liver or gall bladder or perhaps both weren't functioning correctly any more. Thus it was that, a very old weak man, he passed away on 7 July, 1975. Just like so many men of action, for whom once brave young men had been killed violently, he died of course *in bed*.

---

where the 'tourists' are virtually all Nazis. Run by an ex-officer of the 'Bodyguard', its guest book records the names of many of those celebrated fugitives, including Degrelle, the Belgian fascist, and, naturally, Skorzeny. The locals insist that when Freddie Forsyth was down-and-out in that region, he picked up his idea for his best-selling novel *The Odessa File* there.

15

Assessment

The Second World War saw the re-emergence of the irregular soldier, who many military historians of the early 20th century had stated was now a thing of the past, a victim of mass conscription and industrialisation. Indeed, the First World War had appeared to show that in trench warfare and everything that went with it there was little place for the individualist in uniform. With the notable exception of Lawrence of Arabia, the annals of the fighting in that terrible holocaust are bare of any figures to compare with those land and airborne commandos of 1939–1945.

In the middle years of the later war the Western Allies found that they were in no position to fight a land battle on any large scale, and the irregular soldier came into his own again; and the history of the Anglo-American armies of those years is replete with such names as David Stirling, Wingate, Frederick, Mac-Lean, Laycock and a half a hundred other brave young British and American officers. In those lean bitter years before the tide of victory turned in the Allies' favour, irregular forces sprang up on all sides, the product of boredom, desperation, and youthful high spirits. Popski's Private Army, Phantom, Long Range Desert Groups, SAS, Special Boat Service, Marine and Army Commandos, OSS – the names of these spirited, adventurous, irregular formations are myriad.

Yet all these organizations had one thing in common: they were all led by men who, although they were dedicated to irregular warfare and were unconventional and imaginative in their approach to battle, were regular officers. Popski, Stirling, Frederick, Wingate had all served in regular army units before the war and whether they were aware of it or not their thinking was dominated by and limited to military objectives. Thus while their units struck out miles behind the military front, their targets were almost exclusively military airfields and aircraft; supply depots and petrol dumps; radar stations and heavy water plants. And even when these units set out to kidnap individuals as did British irregular formations in Crete and Africa, the persons they intended to kidnap were members of the military, for example General Kreipe and Field-Marshal Rommel.

Otto Skorzeny worked differently. He was not a pre-war regular soldier, but a gifted amateur forced into the military by the circumstances of the war and into the Friedenthal 'Hunting Battalions' by the fact that conventional military formations no longer needed him after his health had been weakened by his service in Russia. It is interesting to note, in this context, that he alone of all the gifted commando leaders of the Second World War did not volunteer for service in these irregular formations but was drafted into them. As a result Skorzeny was not constrained to act by the rules of conventional military training or thinking. He was allowed to let his versatile and quick imagination run its full course, envisaging right from the start targets which were not solely military but which were political and economic, such as the Ural war industry project suggested to him by Himmler almost as soon as he took over the Friedenthal assignment.

Ally this un-military approach to the temperament of the 'Bohemian Corporal', as Field-Marshal von Rundstedt called Hitler disdainfully, who scorned the conventional military approach to the problems of war and acted on the basis of 'hunches', and we get an ideal combination, which invariably led to Skorzeny's formations being used for other than strictly military assignments.

Thus with the likeable Skorzeny having the ear of his fellow countryman Adolf Hitler, and it must be remembered that although Mr Churchill had a weakness for irregular military units, no British commando leader ever had the direct access to the British Prime Minister as did Skorzeny to his Leader, it is not surprising that the two of them could pull off two of the most outstanding military-political feats of the whole war: the rescue of the Italian dictator Benito Mussolini and the crushing of the Horthy family's plot to sign a separate peace with the Russians. In both cases Otto Skorzeny's successful execution of the tasks given him by Adolf Hitler meant that he had contributed significantly to the Third Reich's ability to continue the war. It is for this reason that whenever the history of the Second World War is discussed, the vital role that Otto Skorzeny played in it must always be mentioned.

Add to this the awareness of the impact of Skorzeny's eighty-man Stielau Force during the Battle of the Bulge, in which this handful of daring young men wearing American uniforms caused panic, confusion and chaos behind Allied lines, as anyone who was there at that time (including this writer) can testify all too well, and we are forced to the conclusion that Skorzeny is not only of historical importance, but that he also has a lesson for our own time.

Ever since the advent of nuclear weapons, military thinking throughout the world has seemingly become set in rigid categories.

The political-military approach used by Otto Skorzeny in the Second World War offers a viable alternative. Most of his contemporary military commanders, Axis and Allied, were unwary victims or willing purveyors of archaic military doctrines, in particular the age-old one which states that the function of an army is to destroy the military power of its opponent. For most military men this destruction of military power had to be executed on the field of battle. Skorzeny, perhaps unwittingly, saw that this was not necessarily so. Military power could be destroyed in the person of one man, especially if that one man was a dictator who did not delegate his authority to his subordinates so that if he were 'dealt with', the military machine would be without a head.

Particularly in the case of Admiral Horthy and his son, Skorzeny showed that the attack on the individual, if carried out swiftly and decisively enough, could shock both politicians and generals into stunned inactivity for long enough for him to carry out his aims, in this case the maintenance of Hungary's contribution to the German cause.

Today the 'Skorzeny' theory of the conduct of war by kidnapping and even assassination, and after all the murder of one man is more acceptable than that of hundreds of millions as would be the case in an all-out atomic war, offers a viable and perhaps more humane alternative to the bitter, protracted, guerrilla type of war or the mass slaughter of a conventional or conventional-nuclear war. This is the lesson that Otto Skorzeny, that genial soldier-of-fortune, still has for our time and if we believe in Victor Hugo's statement that 'no army can withstand the strength of an idea whose time has come', perhaps it is a lesson that our military leaders should learn.

Bibliography

Principal Interviews

SS Obersturmbannführer Otto Skorzeny
SS Obersturmbannführer Jochen Peiper
SS Obersturmbannführer Gerd Bremer
SS Standartenführer Albert Fray
General der Artillerie Walter Farnbacher
General der Fallschirmtruppe Kurt Student
Oberst der Abwehr Klaus Ritter
Oberst der Abwehr Hermann Giskes.
Herr Hermann Heim (Secretary to Martin Bormann)

Published works

R. Collier, *Duce*, Popular Library, 1971
C. Foley, *Commando Extraordinary*, Ballatine Books, 1955
R. Gehlen, *The Service*, Popular Library, 1972
G. Infield, *Skorzeny*, Heritage Press, 1968
B. Marshall, *The White Rabbit*, Houghton Mifflin, 1953
J. Mader, *Jagd nach dem Narbengsicht*, Deutscher Militärverlag, 1962
O. Skorzeny, *Skorzeny Secret Missions* (translated from the German) Dutton, 1950
J. Toland, *The Last 100 Days*, Hutchinson, 1960
A. Petacco, *Dear Benito, caro Winston*, Mondadori, 1985
G. Conrini, *La Valigia di Mussolini. Documenti segreti dell'ultima fuga del Duce*, Mondadori, 1987